Scott Foresman
Reading
New Beginnings

New Beginnings

You + Me = Special

Zoom In!

Side by Side

Scott Foresman

About the Cover Artist
Where John Sandford lives in Michigan, there are lots of small animals such as squirrels and chipmunks, but when he is painting an animal he thinks about a person he knows. He says that thinking of a particular person as he works gives his animals personality.

ISBN 0-673-62159-6

4 5 6 7 8 9 10-VH-06 05 04 03 02 01 00

Scott Foresman Reading

New Beginnings

Program Authors

Peter Afflerbach

James Beers

Camille Blachowicz

Candy Dawson Boyd

Deborah Diffily

Dolores Gaunty-Porter

Violet Harris

Donald Leu

Susan McClanahan

Dianne Monson

Bertha Pérez

Sam Sebesta

Karen Kring Wixson

Scott Foresman

Editorial Offices: Glenview, Illinois • New York, New York
Sales Offices: Reading, Massachusetts • Duluth, Georgia • Glenview, Illinois
Carrollton, Texas • Menlo Park, California

Contents

You + Me = Special

Celebrity Author

David A. Adler

CYNTHIA RYLANT
POPPLETON
and Friends

Illustrated by MARK TEAGUE

4

Unit 1

Contents

Zoom In!

Side by Side

Unit 3

Celebrity Author

David A. Adler

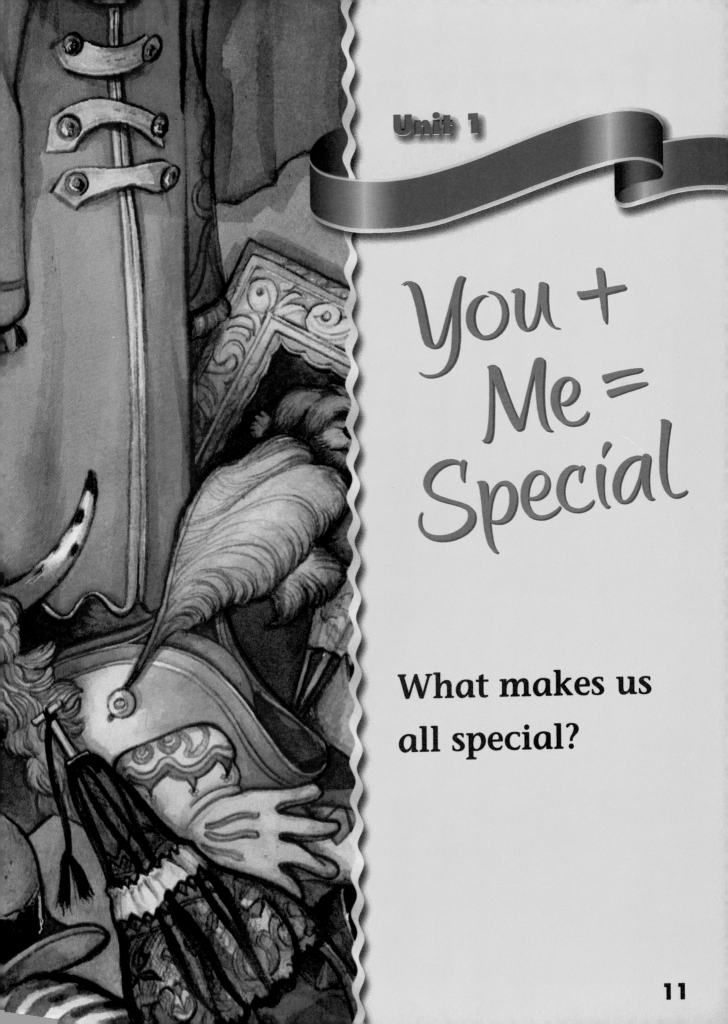

You + Me = Special

What makes us all special?

Franny and Ginny

by Pat Cummings
illustrated by Fred Willingham

Franny spied a ladybug
Sitting in the sun.
So her sister Ginny
Went and found another one.

"Franny, does your ladybug
Have three spots or two?"
Franny said to Ginny,
"Must you do just as I do?"

Franny got her pencils out.
She found some paper too.
Then she said to Ginny,
"Please, do not do just as I do."

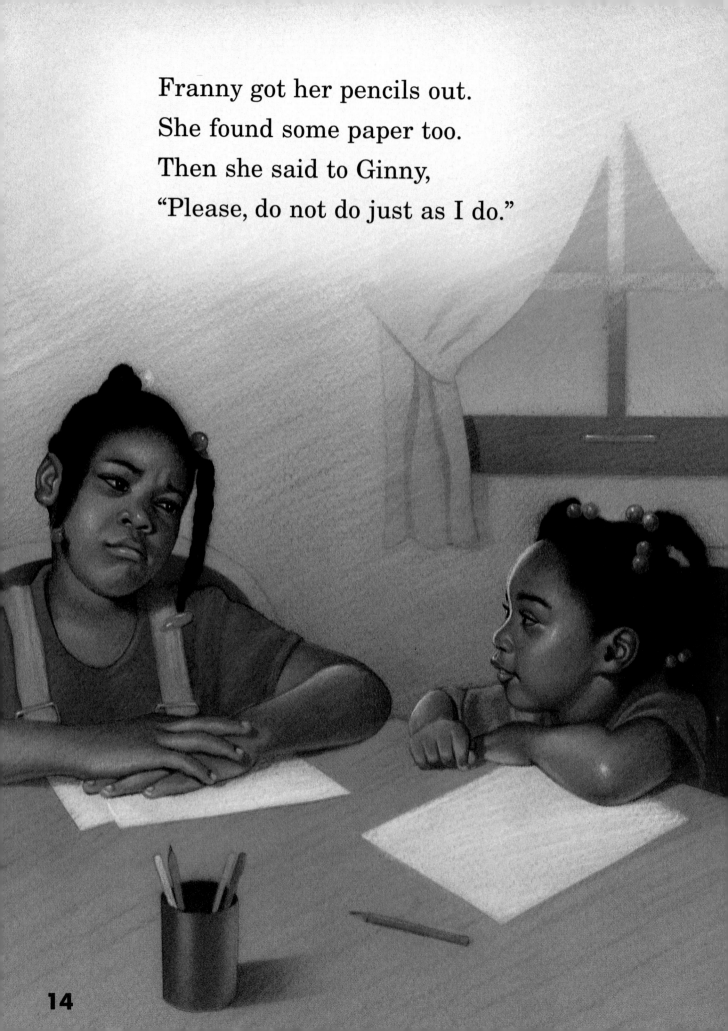

Franny drew a flower.
Then Ginny drew one too.
So Franny said to Ginny,
"MUST you do just as I do?"

Ginny sprang up and left the room,
And Franny drew a strange green cow.
Then Franny had to wonder,
"Could Ginny need me now?"

Franny ran all through the house.
She found Ginny in her bed.
There she was, fast asleep,
With a picture by her head.

Ginny had made a picture
Of two sisters hand in hand.
As Franny saw what Ginny had done,
She now could understand.

Franny said to Ginny,

"I LOVE your picture. It is true."

Then she gave her sis a hug and said,

"I truly love YOU too."

Daddy, Could I Have an Elephant?

by Jake Wolf
illustrated by Marylin Hafner

"Daddy," said Tony. "I need a pet."

"You do?" said his father.

"Yes," said Tony.

"What kind?" said his father.

"Could I have an elephant?" said Tony.

"An elephant?" said his father.
"Where would you keep it?"

"Here in the apartment," said Tony.

"How would you feed it? Where
would it drink?"

"It could drink out of the bathtub,"
said Tony. "We could send out
for Chinese."

"What if it got lonely?" said his father.
"Elephants live in herds."

"We could get another elephant
to keep it company," said Tony.

"How would we move the
elephants up here to the
third floor?" said his father.

"Like pianos," said Tony.
"Pull them on ropes."

"I don't think elephants would fit through the window," said his father.

"We could try," said Tony.

"What if they got stuck?" said his father. "People would talk about us."

"What would they say?" said Tony.

"They'd say we're that family with the elephants sticking out the windows."

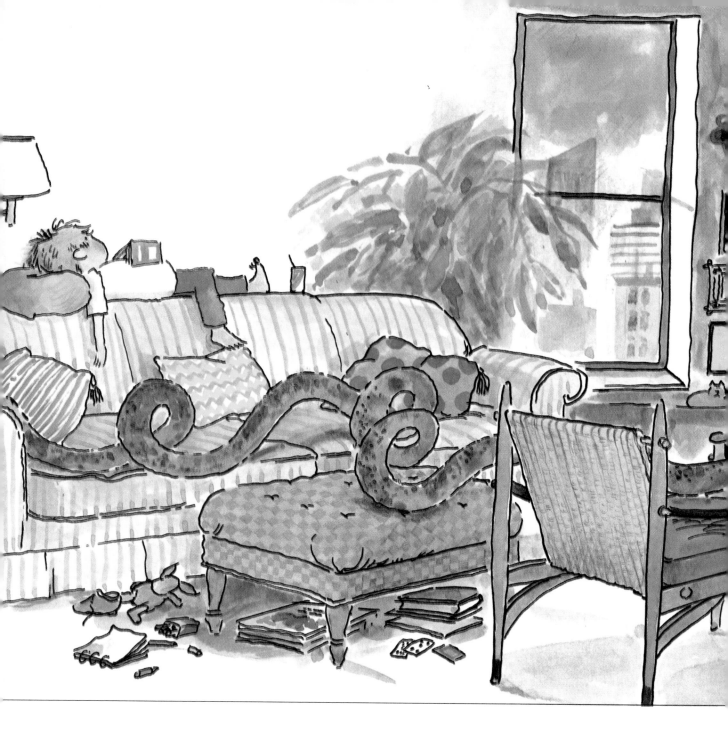

"Well, how about a python?" said Tony.
"One that's twenty feet long."

"Where would you keep it?"
said his father.

"Some of it on the sofa," said Tony,
"the rest of it on chairs."

"Where would *we* sit?" said his father.

"A flock of woolly sheep would be nice," said Tony. "They could keep us warm at night."

"Sheep go *B-A-A-A* when you're trying to sleep," said his father.

"Not if they're asleep too,"
said Tony. "We could give them
a definite bedtime."

"What if they woke up early?"
said his father.

"I know what," said Tony.

"What?" said his father.

"We could fill the living room with water."

"And then?" said his father.

"We could get a dolphin," said Tony,
"and a baby whale."

"Both?" said his father.

Tony and his father were quiet for a while.

"Maybe we should get something small," said Tony.

"What could that be?" said his father.

"Puppies are small," said Tony.

"Just what I was thinking," said
his father.

About the Author
Jake Wolf

Jake Wolf is the pen name of a famous writer and illustrator of children's books. "Thank you for asking," said Mr. Wolf, "but I don't want anyone to know who I really am."

Mr. Wolf enjoys his privacy. He wants to remain a mystery. What do you think about this?

About the Illustrator
Marylin Hafner

Marylin Hafner has illustrated many books. If you read *Ladybug* magazine, you probably have seen Ms. Hafner's work. She creates stories about a girl named Molly and her cat, Emmett.

Let's Talk

If you could have any animal from the story as a pet, which one would you choose? Why?

Think About It

1. Do the animals really come to Tony's house?

2. Why do you think Tony's father buys him a puppy at the end of the story?

3. Do you think Tony's father will help Tony take care of the puppy?

Draw a Poster About Pet Care

Think of three tips you could give Tony about taking care of a pet. Make a poster that shows these tips. Share it with the class.

The Wobbly People in Ellen's Block House

by David A. Adler
illustrated by Nan Brooks

"Look," Ellen told her best friend Peg.

"I made a house of blocks."

"That's great," Peg said.

Peg found some wobbly people. She put them in the block house. Peg told Ellen, "These are Don, Bob, Beth, and Jenny. These are the people who live in your block house."

Peg played with the wobbly people. She
fed them with a tiny red spoon.

"Here, Don. Taste this. Here, Beth.
Taste this."

Peg made Bob hop and Jenny jog.

Ellen said, "Let me play too."

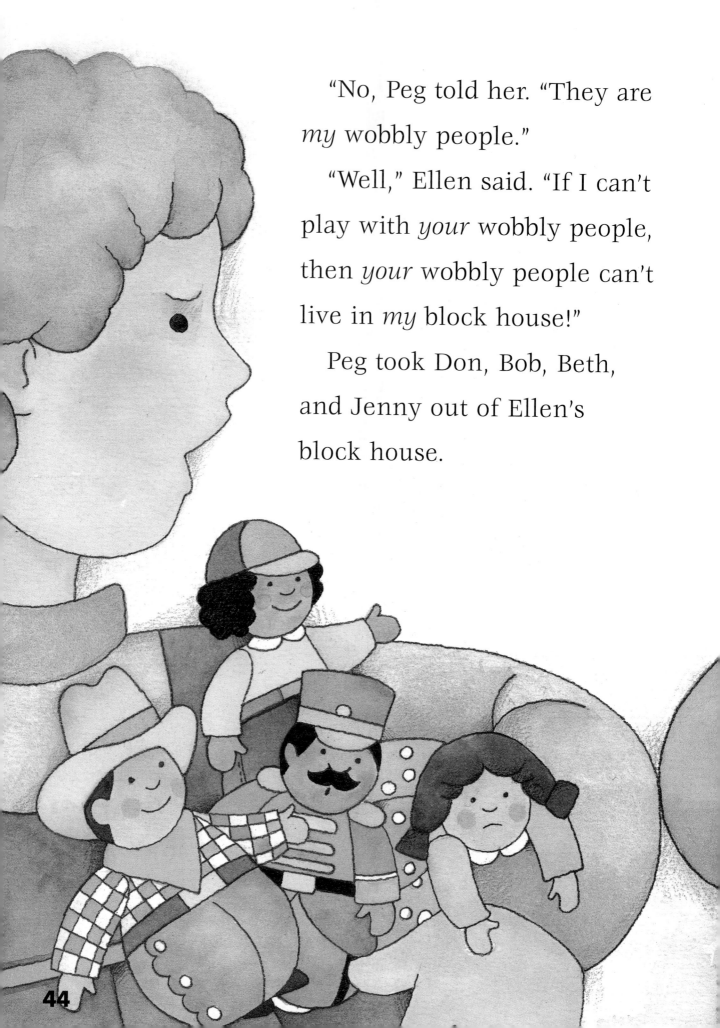

"No, Peg told her. "They are *my* wobbly people."

"Well," Ellen said. "If I can't play with *your* wobbly people, then *your* wobbly people can't live in *my* block house!"

Peg took Don, Bob, Beth, and Jenny out of Ellen's block house.

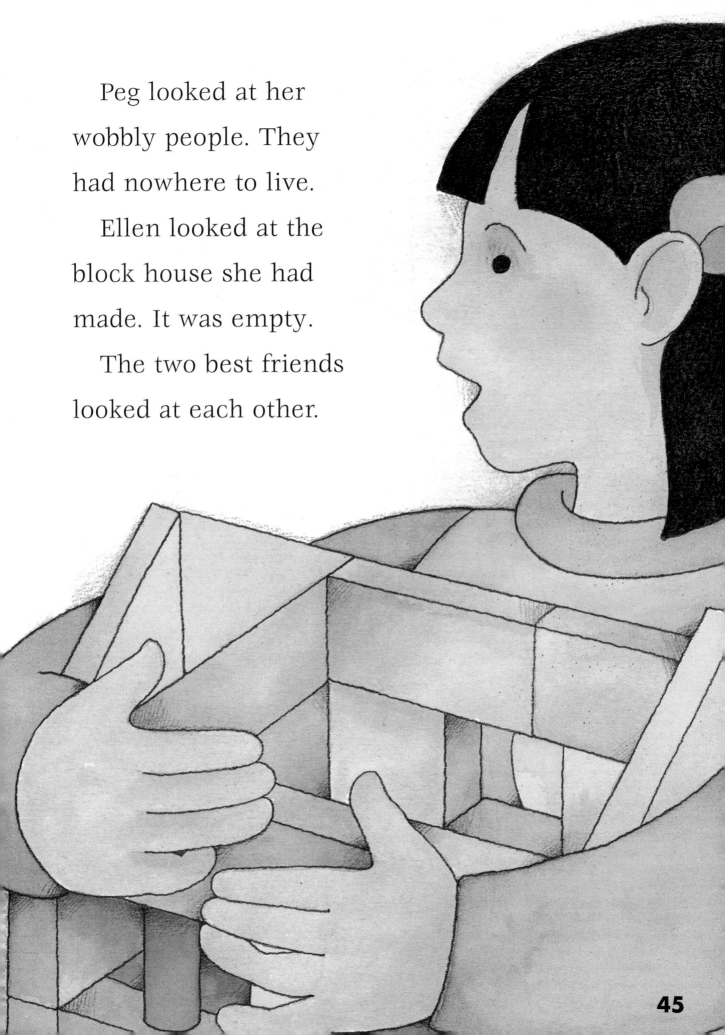

Peg looked at her wobbly people. They had nowhere to live.

Ellen looked at the block house she had made. It was empty.

The two best friends looked at each other.

"I'll share my wobbly people with you,"
Peg said.

"And I'll share my block house with you,"
Ellen said.

Later, Peg's mom gave Peg and Ellen pretzels and fresh hot popcorn. "Thank you," Peg and Ellen said. They shared the pretzels and popcorn.

Poppleton and the Grapefruit

by Cynthia Rylant • illustrated by Mark Teague

One day Poppleton was watching TV. The man on TV said grapefruit made people live longer.

Poppleton hated grapefruit. But he wanted to live longer. He wanted to live to be one hundred.

So he went to the store and
brought home some grapefruit.

He cut it up and took a little taste.
Poppleton's lips turned outside-in.

He took another little taste.
Poppleton's eyes made tears.

He took the tiniest taste
he could possibly take.

Poppleton's face turned green.

Poppleton's friend Hudson knocked at the door.

"Poppleton, why are you all green?" Hudson cried. "And where are your lips?"

"I am eating grapefruit to live longer," said Poppleton. "And it is making me sick."

"Then don't eat it!" cried Hudson.

"But I want to live to be one hundred," said Poppleton.

"With no lips?" asked Hudson.

"What else can I do?" asked Poppleton.

"Wait here," said Hudson.

Soon he was back with a very,
very, very old mouse.

"This is my uncle Bill," said Hudson.
"Uncle Bill, tell Poppleton how you
lived to be one hundred."

Uncle Bill nodded. He leaned
over to Poppleton.

"Friends," he said.

"Friends?" asked Poppleton.

"Friends," said Uncle Bill. "What
did you do with your lips?"

When Uncle Bill and Hudson left,
Poppleton threw all of the
grapefruit away.

And as soon as his lips came back,

he went out to find some friends.

About the Author
Cynthia Rylant

Until she was eight years old, Cynthia Rylant lived in a house with no running water. After college she worked as a waitress. Then she got a job in a library. "And boy, did my life change when I discovered children's books!" she says.

About the Illustrator
Mark Teague

Even as a child, Mark Teague made his own books. When he grew up, he worked in a bookstore. In the store he remembered the fun of making books. He decided to try it again.

"I use a pencil for drawing and a huge eraser for erasing until I get it right," Mr. Teague says.

People

by Charlotte Zolotow
illustrated by Deborah Morse

Some people talk and talk
and never say a thing.
Some people look at you
and birds begin to sing.

Some people laugh and laugh
and yet you want to cry.
Some people touch your hand
and music fills the sky.

Let's Talk

If you could talk to Poppleton, what would you say to him about making new friends?

Think About It

1. Why does Poppleton believe that grapefruit will help him live to be one hundred?

2. How could friends help Poppleton live a long life?

3. What do you think happened when Poppleton went out to find new friends?

Make a Collage

Cut out pictures from magazines that show people doing or eating things that are good for them. Glue your pictures on a piece of paper and share your collage with your class.

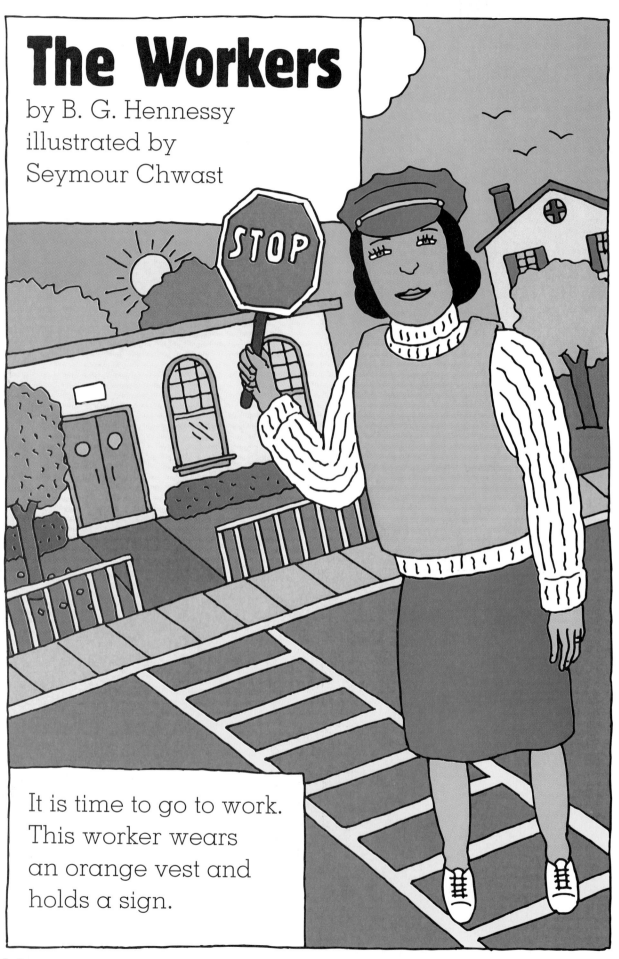

The Workers

by B. G. Hennessy
illustrated by
Seymour Chwast

It is time to go to work.
This worker wears
an orange vest and
holds a sign.

This worker keeps many things clean. He will use a bucket and mop.

This worker wears
a white apron.
She will use a big
spoon and pot.

This worker will make everything ready for the best workers in the world.

Tools

by Ann Morris
photographed by Ken Heyman

A Look at Tools Around the World

Peru

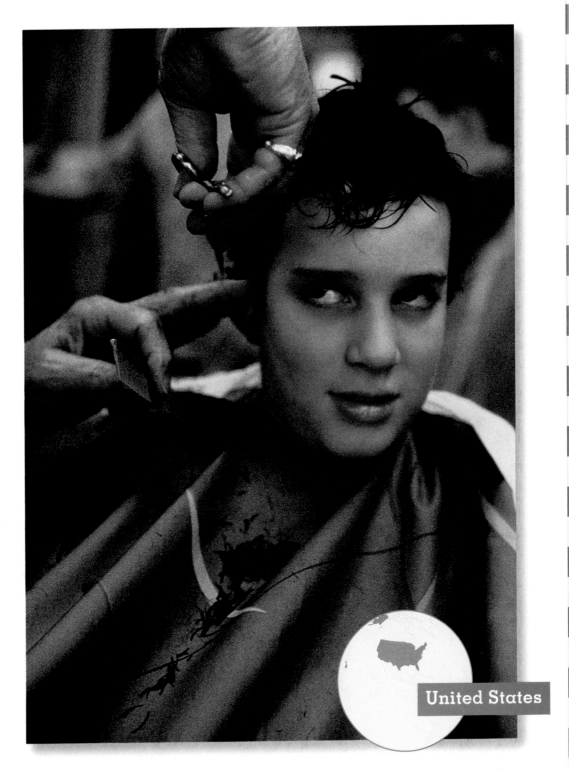

United States

All over the world people use tools.

Tools help us in many ways.

Hong Kong

They help us to cut

and pound

and dig.

Bali

France

We farm with tools.

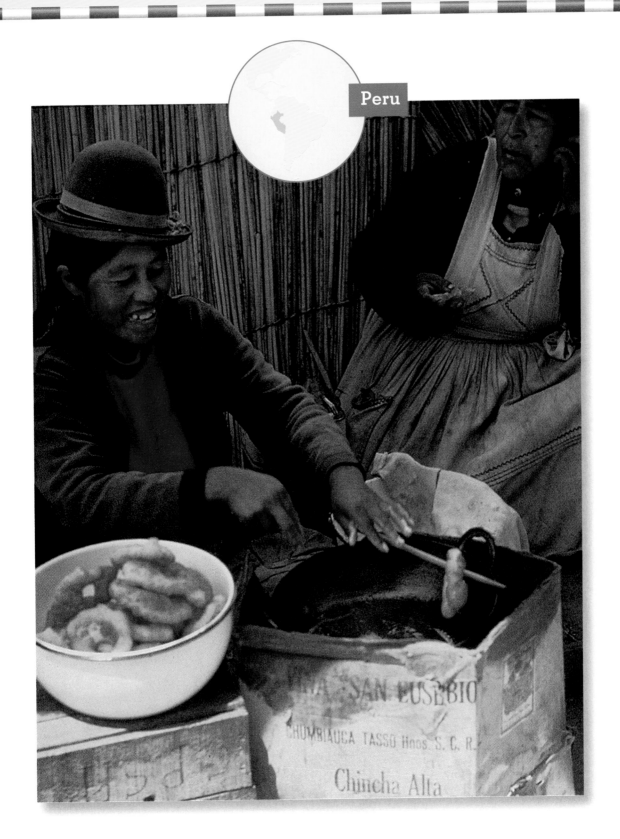

Peru

We cook with tools.

We even eat with tools!

United States

United States

Egypt

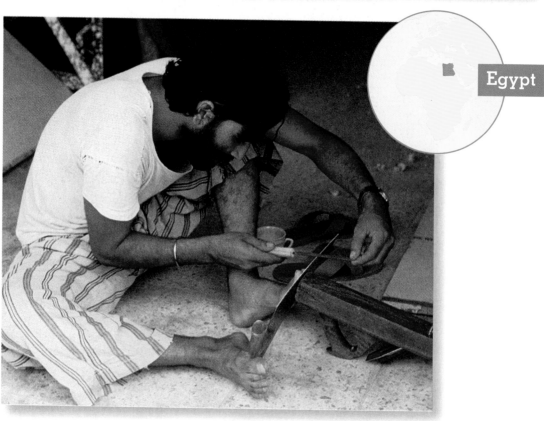

People use tools to make things
and to fix things

Portugal

and to clean.

India

Russia

Tools help us to write and count

and draw and paint.

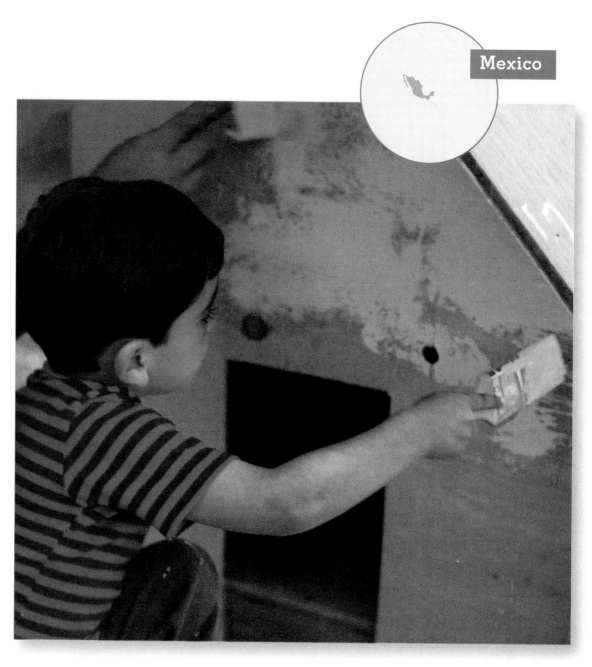

Tools help us with our work.

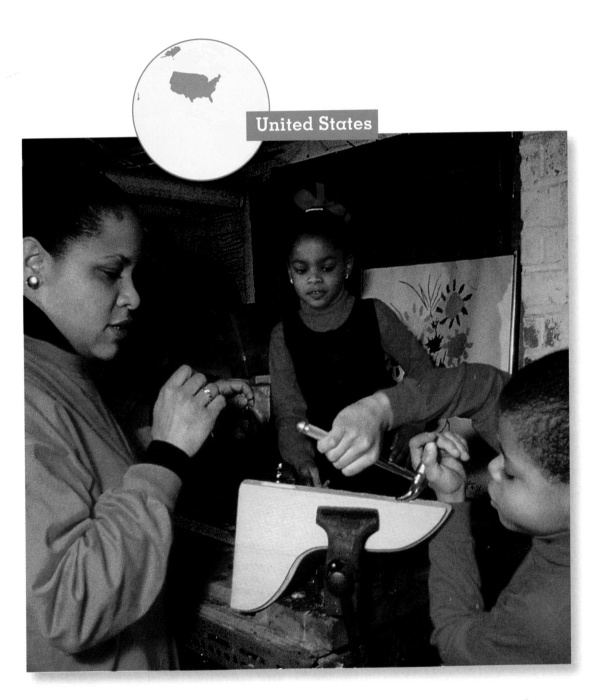

They make our lives easier!

Tools Around the World

Can you find Brazil, Russia, and Egypt?

RUSSIA

FRANCE

PORTUGAL

EGYPT

INDIA

HONG KONG

BALI

85

About the Author and the Photographer

Ann Morris

Author

Ann Morris grew up in New York City. She has always liked learning about people and where they live. She also likes music, cooking, and cats.

Ken Heyman

Ken Heyman grew up in New York City too. He began taking photographs in high school. He still likes to take pictures as he travels.

Photographer

Ann Morris and Ken Heyman have made many books together.

86

Reader Response

Let's Talk

What tools do you use every day? Why do you need them?

Think About It

1. Do people use the same tools everywhere in the world? How do you know?

2. Are more tools used in schools or in homes? Tell why you think so.

3. The author says that tools make our lives easier. How does she show that?

Invent a Tool

Think of a new tool that a person could use. Could you make one from a paper clip, a straw, or something else around you? Draw your new tool. Then try making it!

The Green Leaf Club
News

by G. Brian Karas

Bike Trip to Green Lake

It is spring and all Green Leaf Club members should get out their bikes! We are planning a trip to Green Lake each week this month. It should be an easy ride.

Meet us at the club each Saturday at 9:00 A.M. Bring a lunch and something to drink. Bring a treat too! The trip should take three hours. See you there!

Our Trip To Eagle Peak

Last year we went to Eagle Peak. It was a very long ride. It was very steep too! We stopped to eat in the shade of some green leaves. Then it started to rain!

We had to rush through our picnic lunch. On the way home, our tires sank deep in the mud. When we got home, we were a very tired bunch!

Bike Safety

It is very busy on the streets this time of year. Have fun on your bikes, but please be careful. Watch out for cars and people. Ride at a safe speed.

Don't forget these three rules:

1. Always wear a helmet.

2. Test your brakes.

3. Use hand signals to turn, slow down, and stop.

New Bike Trail Opens!

Beaver Creek Trail is opening! A ribbon
will be cut to open it. We will thank the
people for their hard work. After that, we
will leave for a trail ride.

The new trail is three miles long. It goes through hills and by a creek. We should see lots of beavers along the way. Would you like to join us?

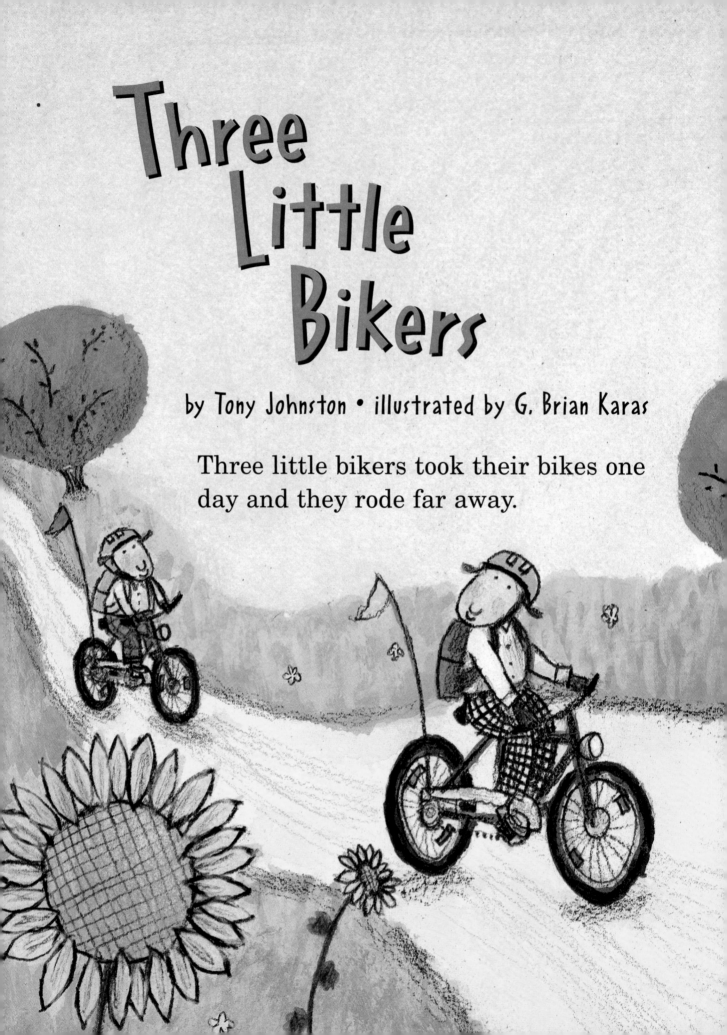

Three Little Bikers

by Tony Johnston • illustrated by G. Brian Karas

Three little bikers took their bikes one day and they rode far away.

The grass was green. The trees were too.
And the sky was blue
as they rode
with their packs on their backs
and three little flags that went
flap, flap, flap
in the wind.

Wind blew in their hair.
It blew everywhere
and puffed their shirts
like little white sails.
And it tickled,
so they giggled
as they rode
with their packs on their backs
and three little flags that went
flap, flap, flap
in the wind.

They rode through gravel
ping, ping, ping.
They rode through dust.
Whisssssh!
They rode through grass
and left their tracks
like three quick little snakes.

They came to a gully,
steep and deep.
Should they? Could they?
Would they cross?
Yes! Yes! Yes!

Watch
for Hill

They raced down the gully
and up again
with their packs on their backs
and three little flags that went
flap, flap, flap
in the wind.

They came to a puddle,
fat with rain.
Should they? Could they?
Would they cross?
Yes! Yes! Yes!

Whooosh!
They splashed
a shiny silver spray.
Then they raced away.

They came to a hill,
green and high.
Should they? Would they?
Could they climb?
Yes! Yes! Yes!

They crept up the hill
with their packs on their backs
and three little flags that went
flop, flop, flop.
Like three little turtles
hurrying up.

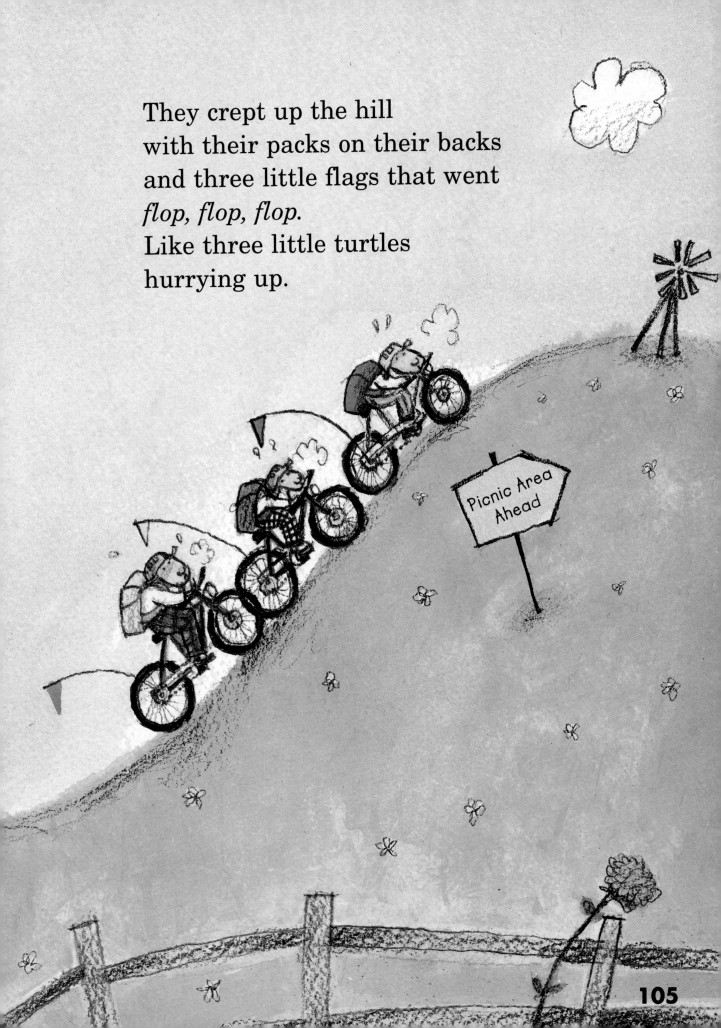

Picnic Area
Ahead

At the very top
they shouted, "Here we are!"
And a voice just like
a voice in a jar
shouted "Are! Are! Are!"

A bird flew up.
So they flew too
and soared like birds
all over the hill
with their arms like wings that went
flap, flap, flap
in the wind.

They rolled all over
like rolling stones.
Grass stuck in their hair.
It stuck everywhere.
And it tickled,
so they giggled
as they rolled.

Then they flopped in the grass
and ate—*chomp, chomp, chomp*—
like three hungry little ants,
till their lunch was gone.
They blew into their bags
and popped them—
Bang! Bang! Bang!

And they sang a loud song
like popping bags,
and they sang a soft song
like birds

till the day got old
and the sky got red
and they knew
it was time to leave.

They looked over the hill,
far, FAR, FAR.
Should they? Could they?
Would they go?
Yes! Yes! Yes!

So—
three little bikers raced down again
with their packs on their backs
and three little flags that went
flap, flap, flap
in the wind.

Gully

Puddle

Hill

As they rode
they sang a song.
And as night came on
their headlights glowed
like three little fireflies
all the way home.

Home

About the Author

Tony Johnston

Tony Johnston was a teacher. She wrote stories for the children in her class. Then she decided to write books for all children to read. Ms. Johnston likes to write in her family room with her dog, Suzi, on her feet!

About the Illustrator

G. Brian Karas

An art teacher helped G. Brian Karas realize that he could be an artist. Since then, he has illustrated over fifty books for children. He believes that creating books "is the most worthwhile thing I can do."

Mr. Karas once was an artist for a large greeting card company.

Reader Response

Let's Talk

Have you ever taken a trip with friends? What are three things that you did on the trip?

Think About It

1. Why are the three bikers like three turtles as they ride up the hill?

2. Why do you think the three little bikers took this trip? How do you know?

3. The three little bikers ride up and down hills. How would the story change if they rode where you live?

Make a Map

Think about all the places the bikers went on their trip. Draw a map showing these places. Add the signs you saw in the story.

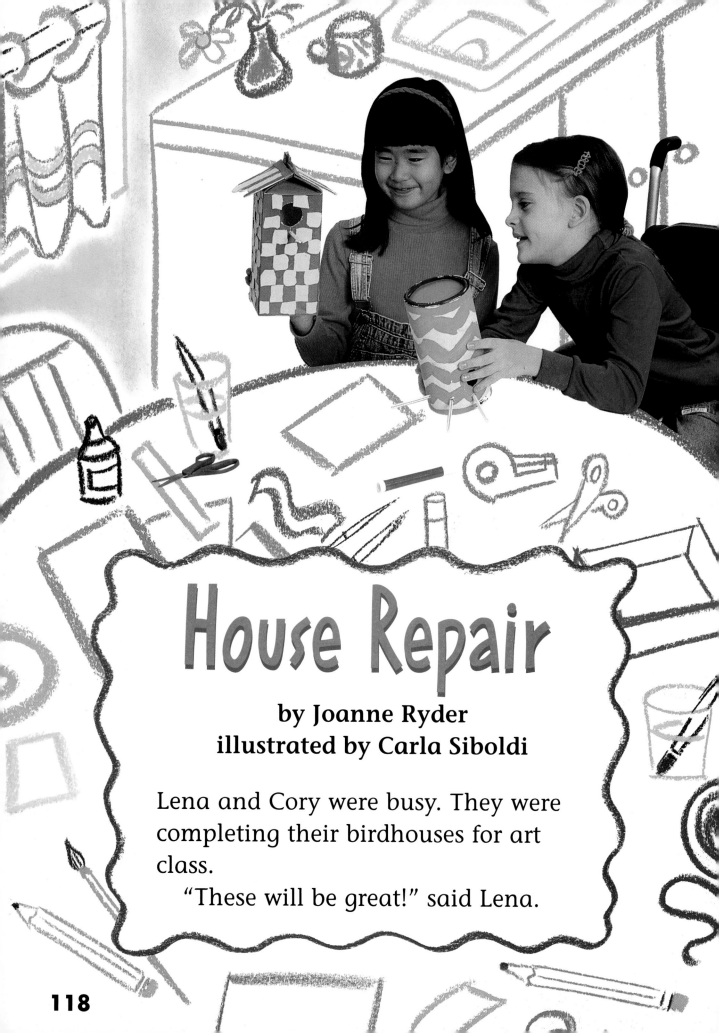

House Repair

by Joanne Ryder
illustrated by Carla Siboldi

Lena and Cory were busy. They were completing their birdhouses for art class.

"These will be great!" said Lena.

Lena was in a big hurry. She wanted to show off her birdhouse. Lena did not see the backpacks on the ground.

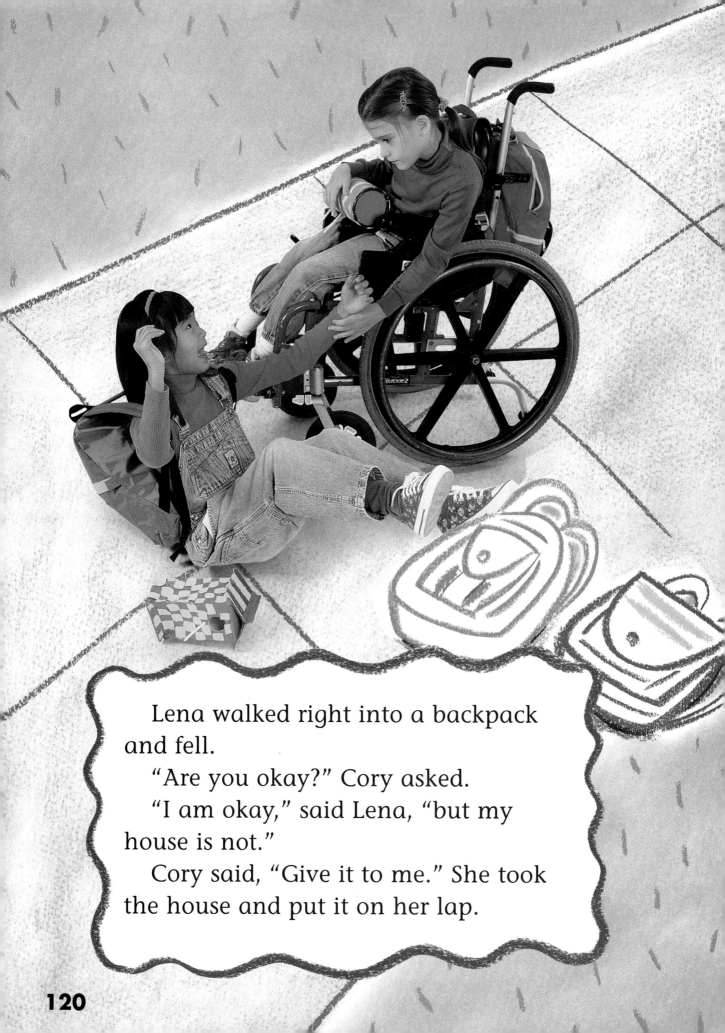

Lena walked right into a backpack and fell.

"Are you okay?" Cory asked.

"I am okay," said Lena, "but my house is not."

Cory said, "Give it to me." She took the house and put it on her lap.

Cory and Lena went to art class.
"I will never be able to repair my house," said Lena.
"Do not worry," said Cory. "We will fix your house."

Cory took off the crushed parts. Then she got busy. She cut and painted and fixed.

"Is this okay?" Cory asked.

"It is more than okay," said Lena.

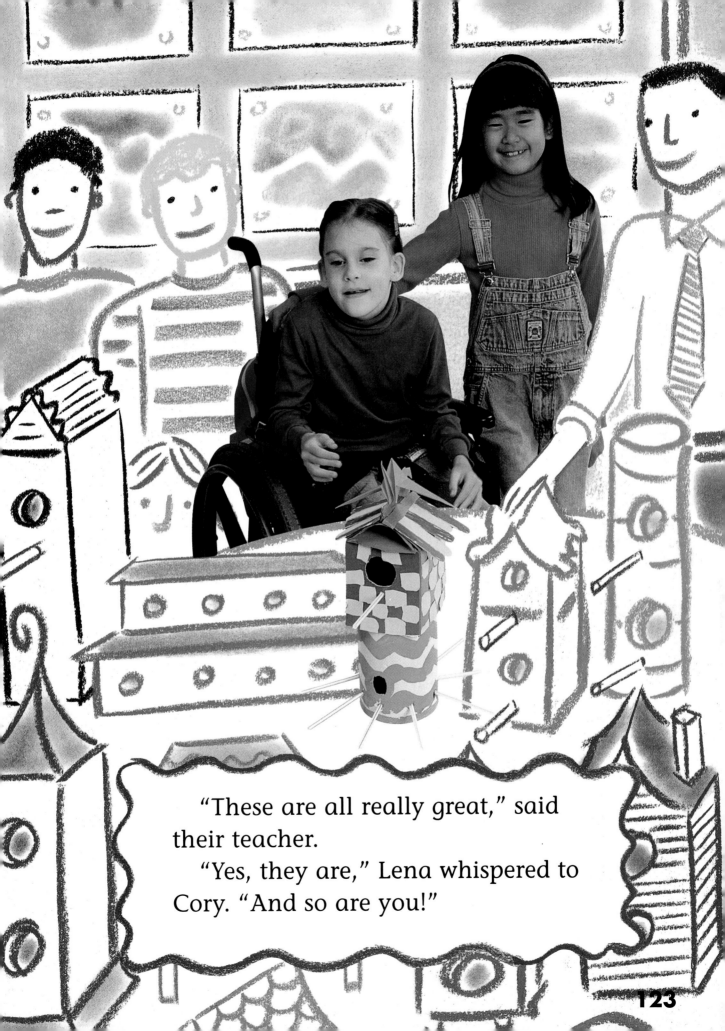

"These are all really great," said
their teacher.

"Yes, they are," Lena whispered to
Cory. "And so are you!"

The Surprise

by Arnold Lobel

It was October.

The leaves had fallen off
the trees.

They were lying on the ground.

"I will go to Toad's house,"
said Frog.

"I will rake all of the leaves
that have fallen on his lawn.
Toad will be surprised."

Frog took a rake
out of the garden shed.

Toad looked out of his window.

"These messy leaves
have covered everything," said Toad.

He took a rake out of the closet.

"I will run over to Frog's house.

I will rake all of his leaves.

Frog will be very pleased."

Frog ran through the woods
so that Toad would not see him.

Toad ran through the high grass
so that Frog would not see him.

Frog came to Toad's house.

He looked in the window.

"Good," said Frog.

"Toad is out.

He will never know

who raked his leaves."

Toad got to Frog's house.
He looked in the window.
"Good," said Toad.
"Frog is not home.
He will never guess
who raked his leaves."

Frog worked hard.

He raked the leaves into a pile.

Soon Toad's lawn was clean.

Frog picked up his rake
and started home.

Toad pushed and pulled on the rake.

He raked the leaves into a pile.

Soon there was not a single leaf

in Frog's front yard.

Toad took his rake

and started home.

A wind came.

It blew across the land.

The pile of leaves

that Frog had raked for Toad

blew everywhere.

The pile of leaves

that Toad had raked for Frog

blew everywhere.

When Frog got home,
he said, "Tomorrow I will
clean up the leaves
that are all over my own lawn.
How surprised Toad must be!"

When Toad got home,
he said, "Tomorrow I will
get to work and rake
all of my own leaves.
How surprised Frog must be!"

That night
Frog and Toad
were both happy
when they each
turned out the light
and went to bed.

About the Author
Arnold Lobel

Arnold Lobel wrote and illustrated almost one hundred books. "One of the secrets of writing good books for children is that you must write books for yourself," he once said.

Watching his children catch frogs and toads one summer gave Mr. Lobel the idea for the characters Frog and Toad. Mr. Lobel said, "I loved those little creatures."

Autumn Leaves

by Leland B. Jacobs

Green leaves,
  Yellow leaves,
    Red leaves, and brown,
      Falling,
        Falling,
          Blanketing the town.
            Oak leaves,
              Maple leaves,
                Apple leaves, and pear,
                  Falling,
                    Whispering,
                      "Autumn's in the air!"
                        Big leaves,
                          Little leaves,
                            Pointed leaves, and round,
                              Falling,
                                Nestling,
                                  Carpeting the ground.

Haiku

by Myra Cohn Livingston
illustrated by Roberta Arenson

One by one, circling
down to earth, these yellow birds,
these frail, falling leaves

Piles of ragged leaves,
flung together, huddle up
against winter's chill.

Let's Talk

Was the ending a surprise?
Why or why not?

Think About It

1. Do Frog and Toad like one another?
   How do you know?

2. What do you think would have happened
   if it had not been a windy day?

3. Why are Frog and Toad happy at the end
   of the story?

Write a Thank-You Note

Think of something nice
that someone has done
for you. Write a thank-you
note to that person.

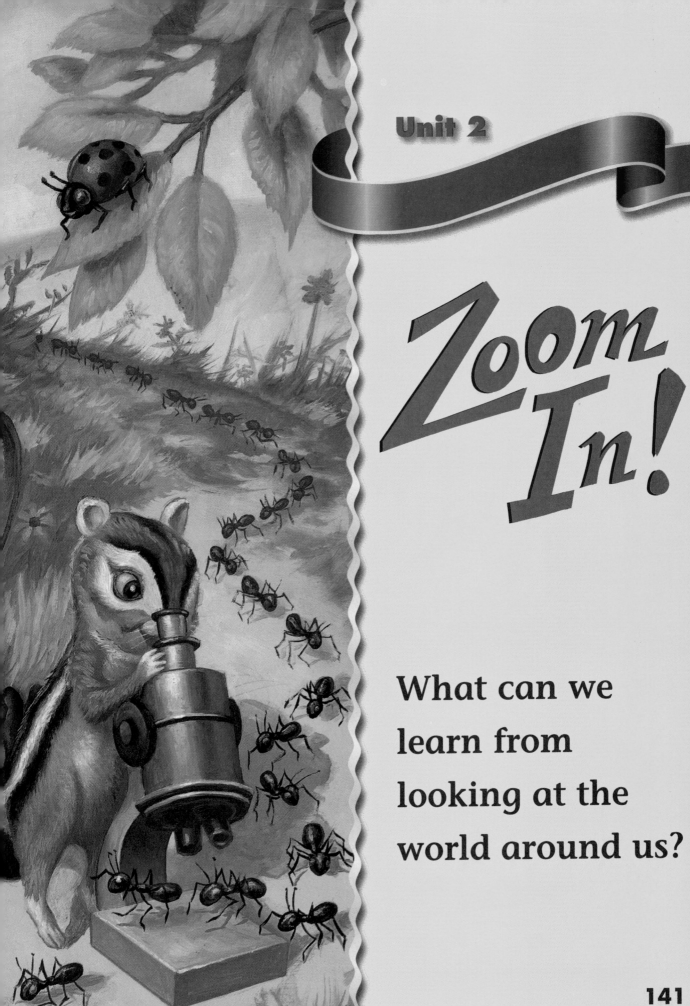

Zoom In!

What can we learn from looking at the world around us?

The Ugly Duckling

by Hans Christian Andersen • retold by Sharon Fear
illustrated by Cheryl Kirk Noll

Mother Duck watches. Her five eggs
are hatching. Four new little
ducklings hatch first. Then one big
duckling hatches.

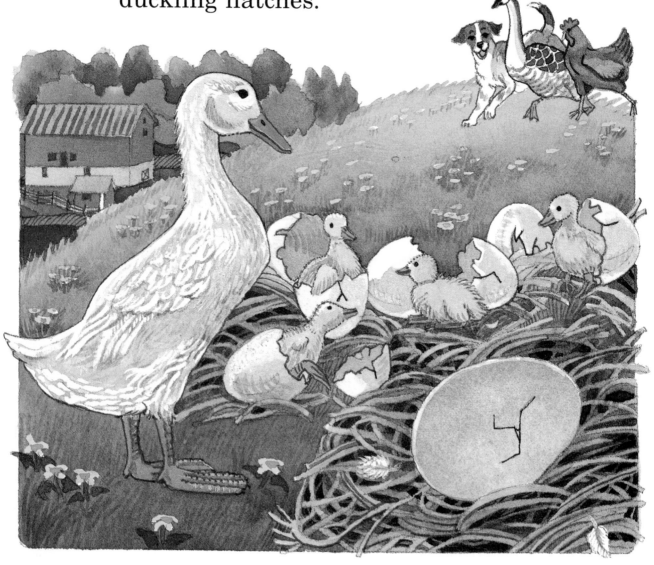

"Four are quite pretty," said Mother
Duck. "But this big one looks very
plain."

"He is an ugly color," said Hen.

"He has ugly feet," added Goose.

"He is ugly all over," said Dog.

"I must be very ugly," said the duckling. "I will not be able to stay. I will go and live by myself."

So the ugly duckling ran away.

His days were sad. He had no one

to play with. His nights were cold.

He had no one to keep him warm.

But time passes.

One day he saw three pretty birds.

They were floating his way.

"Look!" said Hen. "Swans!"

"Beautiful swans!" said Goose.

"Four beautiful swans!" said Dog.

The ugly duckling looks in the water.

He sees . . . four beautiful swans!

And he is one of them!

DUCK

by Angela Royston
photographed by Barrie Watts

In the nest

My mother has laid her eggs
in this nest. She sits on
them to keep them warm.

Inside each egg a new duckling
is growing. This one is me. I am
just beginning to hatch.

Just hatched

I have chipped away my shell,
and now I am pushing myself out.

At last I am out of my shell.

I can see, hear, stand, and walk.
I can cheep too. Where
is my mother?

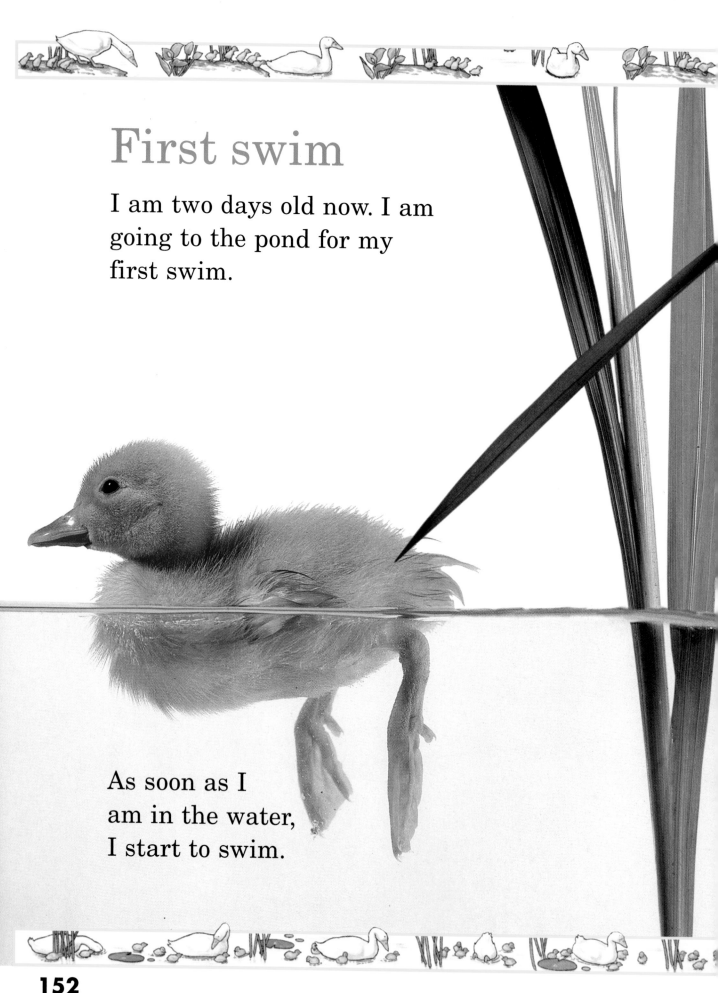

First swim

I am two days old now. I am going to the pond for my first swim.

As soon as I am in the water, I start to swim.

I use my webbed feet to paddle through the water.

Feeding

I am one week old and getting bigger. I like to explore everything.

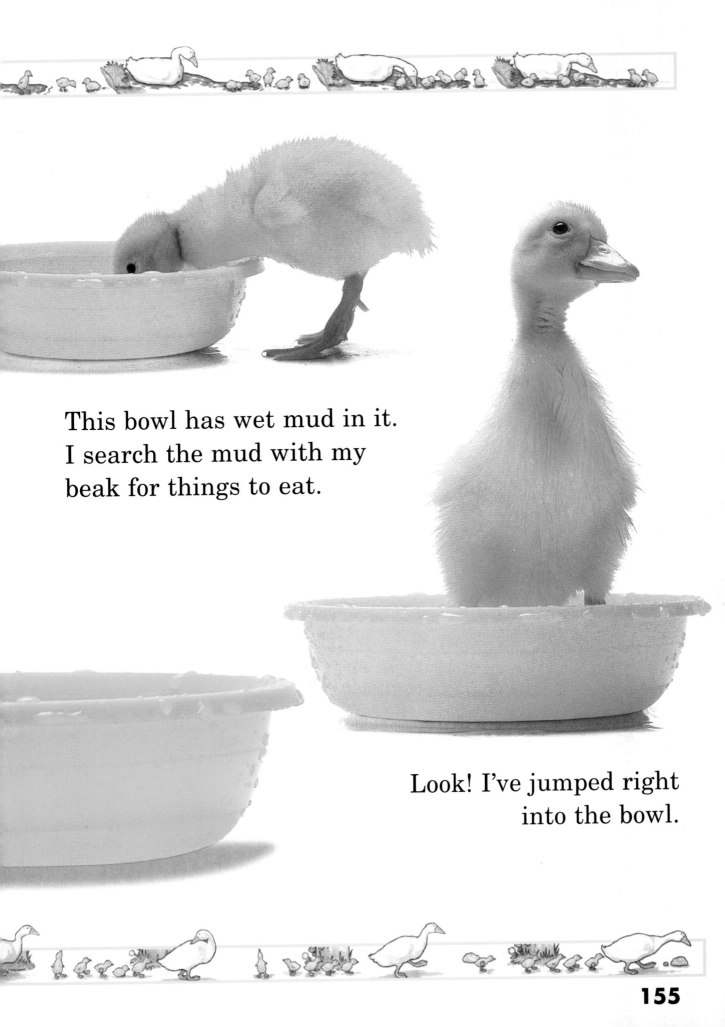

This bowl has wet mud in it.
I search the mud with my
beak for things to eat.

Look! I've jumped right
into the bowl.

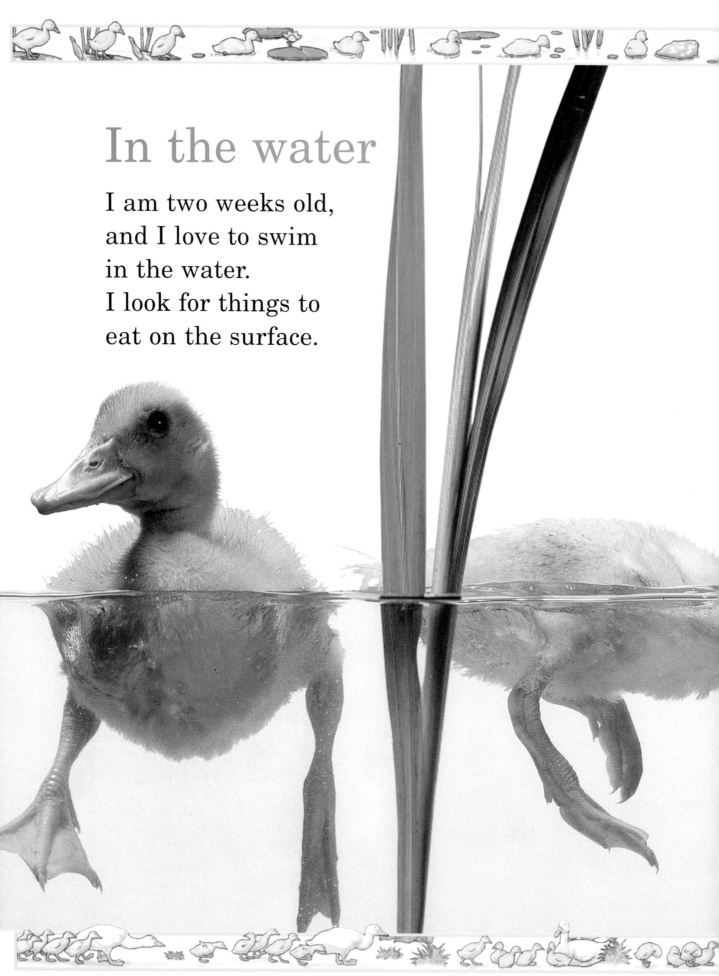

In the water

I am two weeks old,
and I love to swim
in the water.
I look for things to
eat on the surface.

I shake the water off my body.

New feathers

I am three weeks old.
My yellow down is
falling out, and new
white feathers are
beginning to grow.

I stay close to the other
ducklings.
Our mother watches
out for danger.

Sometimes we huddle together. Our feathers help to keep us warm.

Nearly grown up

I am six weeks old and nearly grown up.

All my feathers are white,
and my wings are big
and strong.

See how much I have
grown. This bowl is small,
but it seemed big when
I first jumped into it.

See how I grew

The egg

One hour old

Two days old   Seven days old   Two weeks old

Three weeks old   Six weeks old

About the Author
Angela Royston

Angela Royston has written many animal stories. She often writes about farm animals. Ms. Royston learns a lot when she writes. "I always become interested in the subjects of the books I work on," she says.

About the Photographer
Barrie Watts

Barrie Watts spends time in Great Britain. The pictures Watts takes are often of animals and plants. They appear in many books and magazines. The subjects of books by Barrie Watts can be as tiny as a fly or a honeybee or as large as a redwood tree.

Let's Talk

What week in the duck's life interested you the most? Tell why.

Think About It

1. How does a duck change as it grows?

2. What does a duck need to learn how to do?

3. Compare the duck at two weeks old and at six weeks old. What has changed? What hasn't changed?

Make a Chart

Pretend that you want to buy a duck. How can you tell a duck's age? Make a chart that shows three stages in a duck's life.

Eye Spy

by Pat Cummings
illustrated by Chris Powers

Mrs. Bright waited for the whole class
to quiet down. "Thank you, Dwight," she
said. "My, your frog farm was very nice.
Now, I have an idea. Why don't you carry
your frog farm outside? The frogs might
like it there."

"OK," said Dwight. "I might find them some bugs first. My frogs *love* to eat bugs."

Mrs. Bright smiled. Then she said, "All right. Who is next? Ida?"

Ida had to carry her things slowly because she wanted to keep some of them hidden. She knew everyone would try to peek. Ida put three pictures up against the board. She put a bag on the floor nearby.

"Try to guess what each picture is," Ida said to the whole class. "I don't think you will get them right," she giggled.

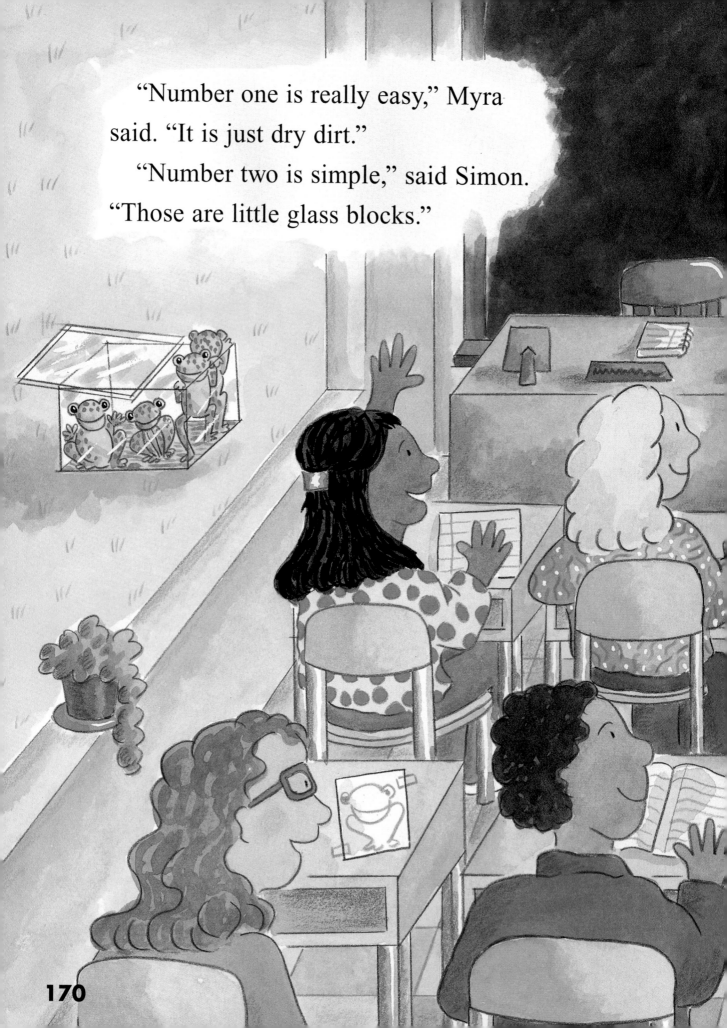

"Number one is really easy," Myra said. "It is just dry dirt."

"Number two is simple," said Simon. "Those are little glass blocks."

Dwight got up because he wanted a closer look. "Why, number three is a fuzzy cotton ball!" he said.

Ida picked up the bag. She pulled out a hand lens and a telescope.

Ida held the hand lens over her arm. "This goes with number one."

"My, oh my!" said Michael. "This is not dirt. This is skin really close up!"

Next Ida took out a packet of sugar. She put some under the class microscope.

"Hey!" laughed Simon. "The glass blocks are really bits of sugar!"

"Now, this goes with number three," said Ida. She pointed the telescope out the window. "Tell me what you see, Dwight."

"Yikes!" yelled Dwight. "I see my whole frog farm about to run across the playground!"

Seeing

by Joanna Cole
illustrated by Neesa Becker

Is your eyeball
really a ball?
Yes!
Most of your eye
is hidden inside
your skull.

Here is what your
whole eye looks like.
Each of your eyes
has an opening to
let in light.
That opening is
called the pupil.

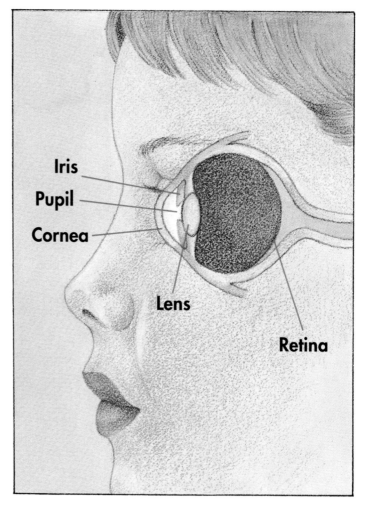

Dim the lights.

Look at your eyes in a mirror.

Are your pupils big?

Now turn on a bright light.

Did you see your pupils get smaller?

Your pupils get bigger and smaller to
let in just the right amount of light.

Your eyes are made to see.

How do they work?

Look at a hat.

Light bounces off the hat and goes into your eye.

The light hits the back of your eyeball.

A picture of the hat is made there.

Nerves—like wires—carry
messages about the picture
from the back of your eye
to special places in your brain.
You need your brain *and* your
eyes to see.

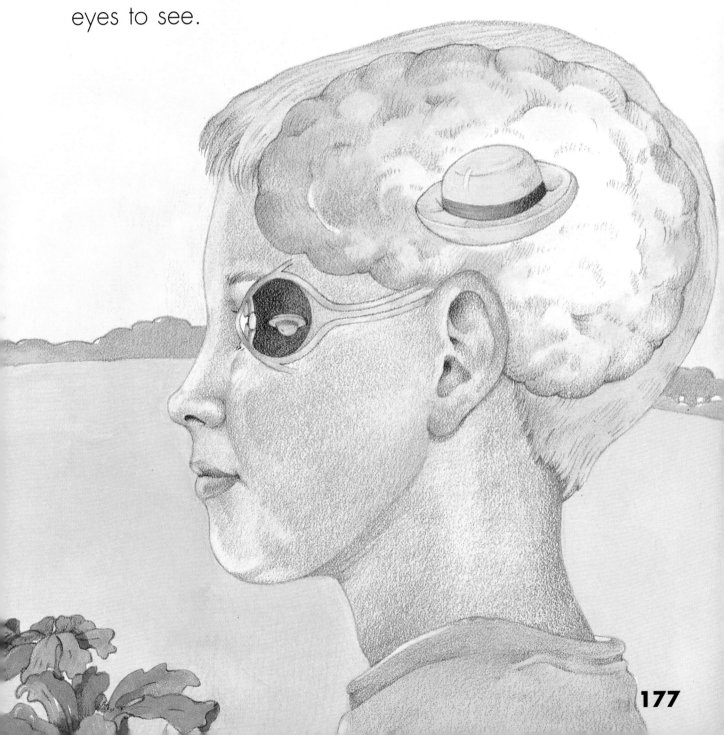

Sometimes your eyes see things
that don't make sense.
Then your brain tries
to make sense of them.

You see a friend coming down the street. While he is still far away, hold up your thumb. Your eyes say that he looks *smaller* than your thumb! But your brain is not fooled. Your friend only looks small because he is far away. You know that he is still big.

Sometimes you *can* fool your brain.

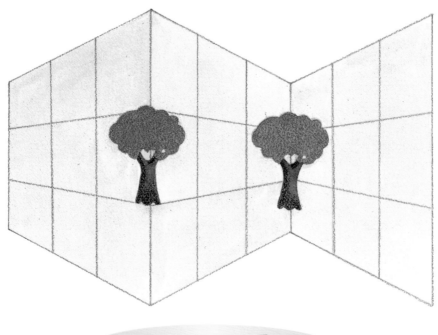

Try This

Look at the picture. Which tree is bigger?

Did you say the one on the right?

No! Both are the same size.

Measure them and see.

Why does one tree seem bigger?

Because the artist drew the picture with lines that make the tree on the right seem farther away. Your brain acts the way it did when you saw your friend down the street. It tells you the tree on the right is bigger than it really is.

Sometimes you can see two pictures in one.

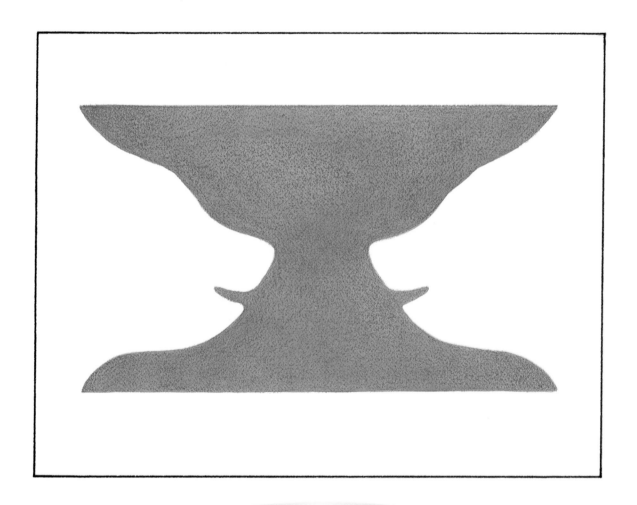

In this picture, do you see a green vase? Or do you see two white dogs looking at each other? You may see one picture, and then the other. But your brain cannot see both pictures at once.

About the Author
Joanna Cole

Joanna Cole began writing stories when she was a child. She also enjoyed drawing pictures to go with her stories.

Ms. Cole always loved writing about science more than anything else. Today, she is well known for her science books. In fact, she is the author of the Magic School Bus books.

Reader Response

Let's Talk

Have your eyes ever fooled you? Tell about it.

Think About It

1. What are some ways that your brain tricks you?

2. Find your iris and pupil. What do they do?

3. What would happen if your pupils did not get bigger or smaller?

Eye Exam

Pretend that you have to teach a friend about how the eyes work. How would you do it? Write a plan and show it to your friend.

Furry Mouse

by Kana Riley
photographed by John Moore

At first, it is dark inside the box.
Furry Mouse looks around. All she
can see is a little light that shines
through holes in the lid.

Then the lid opens. Light comes
in. Furry Mouse opens her eyes
wide and turns.

Furry Mouse wiggles her nose.
She smells food—seeds, carrots,
and one other thing. She wiggles
her nose again. Strawberries! Yum!
Furry Mouse loves strawberries.

Something stirs. Furry Mouse
perks up her ears. What does she
hear?

Furry Mouse looks one way,
then another. She creeps ahead
until she is almost out of the box.

Wood chips brush over her fur.

They feel good under her paws.

She looks around her new home.

Look! It has a water bottle and a dish for food. This is perfect.

Furry Mouse is thirsty. But first she must look around some more.

Something stirs again! Furry Mouse turns to look. A ball of fur races up the ladder. It is another mouse! He jumps down and almost lands on Furry Mouse.

He scurries around and under the wood chips.

Then he hops up on the wheel.

He moves around and around.

Furry Mouse watches. It looks like
fun! She waits for her turn.

Yes, this is a good home.

TWO MICE

by Lynn Reiser

Once there were two mice
who lived beside a window.

One lived
inside the window,
in a cage on top of a
bookshelf.
One lived outside
the window,
in a mouse hole
under a rosebush.

The inside mouse
ate mouse food from a bowl,
drank water from a bottle,
and ran around a wheel.

The outside mouse
ate strawberries
and acorns,
drank raindrops
from rose leaves,
and ran
in and out
the mouse hole
and up and down
and around
the rosebush.

One night
the window was open.
The outside mouse ran in.

The two mice
ate mouse food from the bowl,
drank water from the bottle,
and ran around the wheel.

One mouse
was content.
One mouse was
ready for more.

The outside mouse ran out.
The inside mouse followed.

The two mice ate a strawberry—
and a snake almost ate them.

They nibbled an acorn—and a raccoon
almost nibbled them.

They drank raindrops
from a rose leaf—

and an owl almost
carried them off to her nest.

One mouse
was ready for more.
One mouse
was ready for a nap.

The window was open.
The inside mouse ran in.

The outside mouse
did not follow.
The outside mouse ran
in and out
and up and down
and around,
playing
"catch me if you can"
with the snake
and the raccoon
and the owl.

The inside mouse
took a nap.

MORAL

What thrills one
tires another.

Lynn Reiser

Lynn Reiser likes animals. She likes to write about animals too. In fact, she has written many animal stories. You may enjoy reading her other books about cats and dogs. Ms. Reiser also likes to paint. She painted the pictures for the story *Two Mice*.

Let's Talk

Would you rather be the outside mouse or the inside mouse? Why?

Think About It

1. Why do the inside mouse and the outside mouse like different things?

2. Why do you think the inside mouse followed the outside mouse outside?

3. How do you think the inside mouse felt when he was outside? Why?

Give Your Reasons

You are the inside mouse. Ask a friend to be the outside mouse. Who can give the best reasons for living inside or outside?

The Old Gollywampus

by Toby Speed
illustrated by Mary Grand Pré

Snake hid low in the woodpile, between rows of oak trees. She was curled in an O. Snake smelled something new. It was not a mouse. It was not a toad.

This smell was cold and crisp.

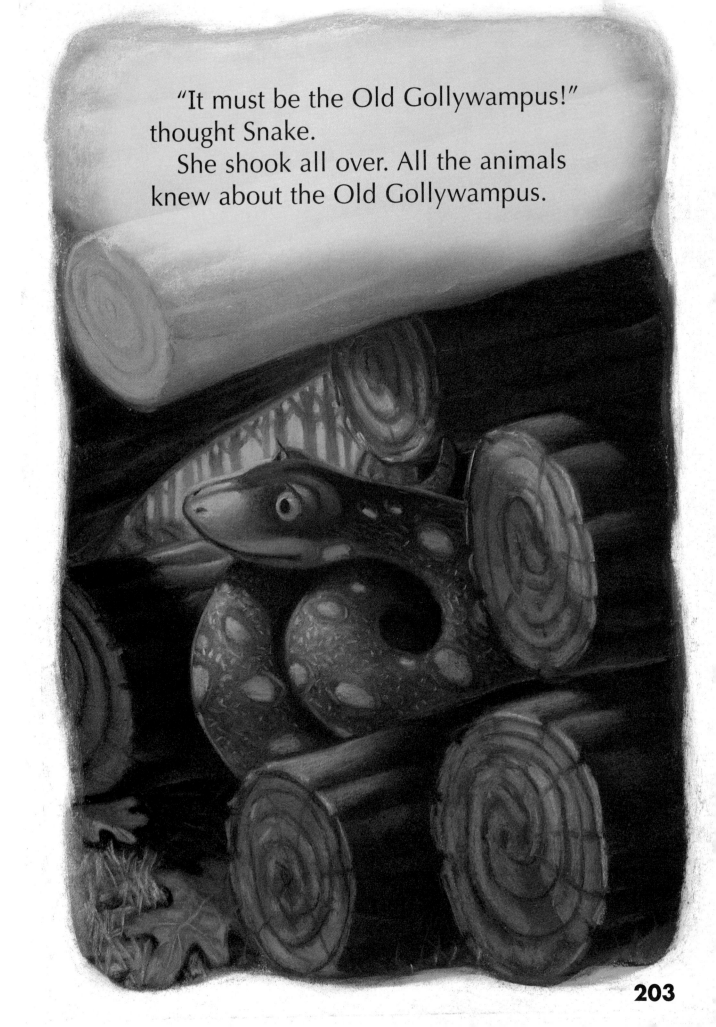

"It must be the Old Gollywampus!"
thought Snake.
She shook all over. All the animals
knew about the Old Gollywampus.

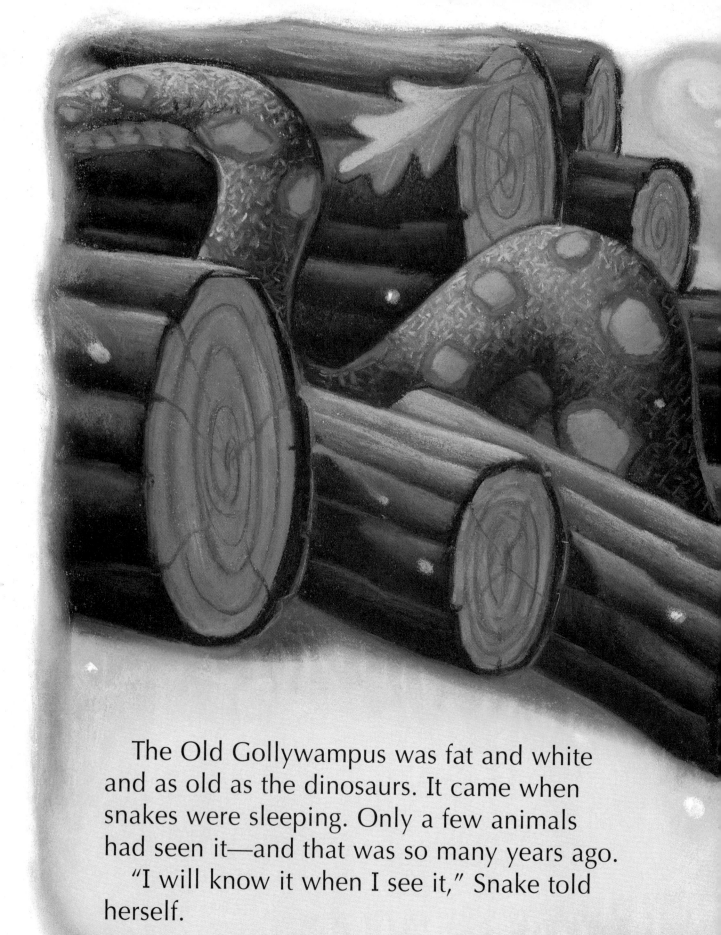

The Old Gollywampus was fat and white and as old as the dinosaurs. It came when snakes were sleeping. Only a few animals had seen it—and that was so many years ago.

"I will know it when I see it," Snake told herself.

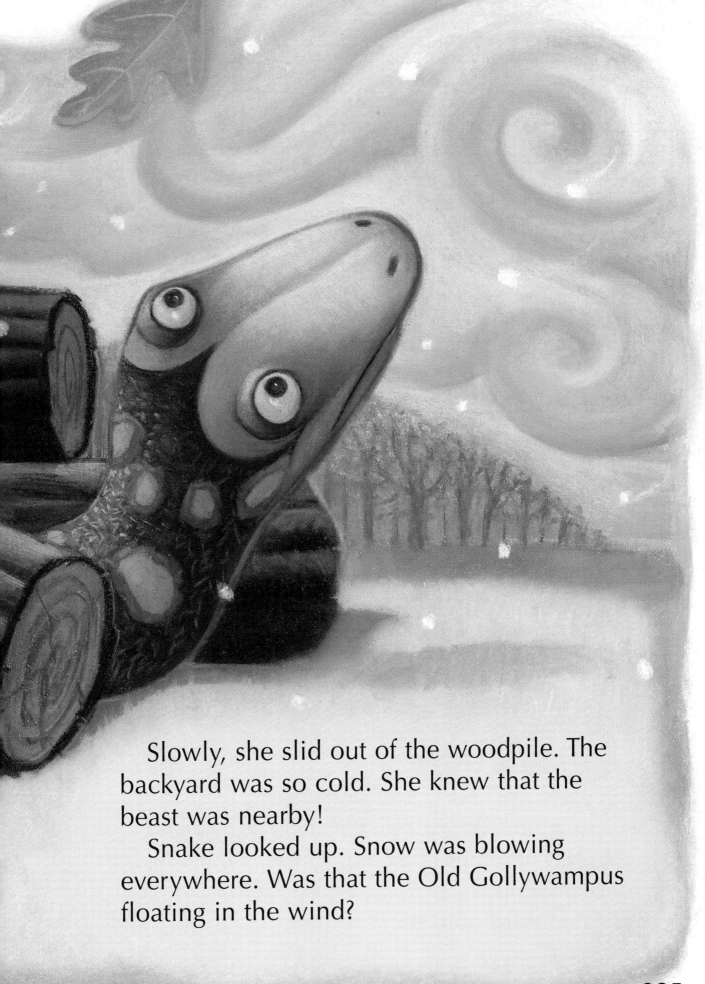

Slowly, she slid out of the woodpile. The backyard was so cold. She knew that the beast was nearby!

Snake looked up. Snow was blowing everywhere. Was that the Old Gollywampus floating in the wind?

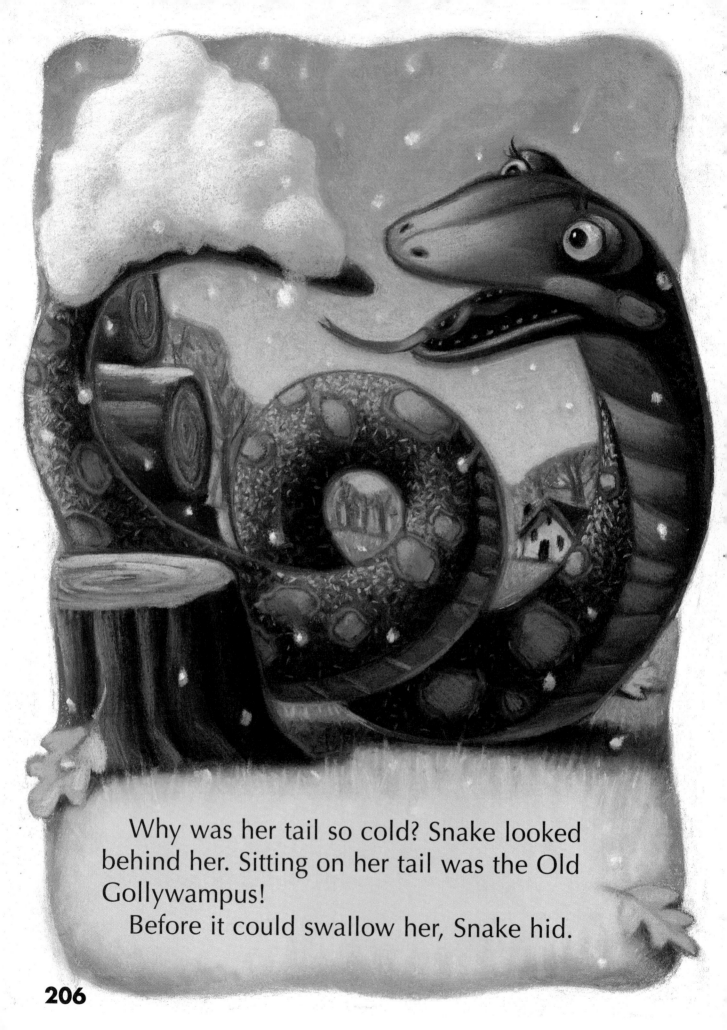

Why was her tail so cold? Snake looked behind her. Sitting on her tail was the Old Gollywampus!

Before it could swallow her, Snake hid.

Snake felt so tired. She curled in an O below the woodpile. The wind was blowing. Snowflakes were floating between the oak trees. Snake slept.

Snakes

by Patricia Demuth
illustrated by Judith Moffatt

Long, long ago, before people knew how to write, they drew pictures on cave walls—pictures of animals.

About a million different animals lived on Earth then. But cave people drew only a few of them.

The snake was one.

People have always found snakes interesting. Why? Maybe it is their shape. Snakes have no arms or legs.

Or maybe it is how they move. Snakes slither and slide on their bellies.

Or maybe it is their skin. Snake skin is made up of lots of little scales. Most snake skin looks slimy, but it isn't. It is very dry.

There are over 2,400 kinds of snakes in the world. They come in many sizes.

The smallest is the thread snake—no bigger than a worm. The giant of all snakes is the anaconda. (You say it like this: an⁄ə kon⁄də.) It can be as long as a school bus and weigh as much as two grown men.

Python 10–30 feet long

Boa 6–18 feet long

Cobra
8–18 feet long

Rat snake 3½–8 feet long

Rattlesnake 3–8 feet long

Garter snake
1½–4 feet long

Other snakes are somewhere in between.

Snakes live almost everywhere: On land, in trees, and underground. In the oceans and lakes.

But snakes don't live near the North Pole or the South Pole. A snake's body can't make its own heat like yours can. So, cold air, cold snake.

But if the air is nice and warm, then the snake is nice and warm too.

Many kinds of snakes can live through cold winters.

How? They find a warm place to hide—in a deep hole, in a cave, or under rocks. Then they go into a deep winter sleep. Here they stay until warm weather returns.

Even when snakes sleep, their eyes are always open. That's because they have no eyelids. A clear cap covers each eye.

Most snakes don't see very well. They can tell if something moves. But this garter snake can barely see the frog that is sitting so quiet and still.

Ribbit, ribbit.
The frog croaks. The garter snake cannot hear the frog. Snakes have no outer ears.

The garter snake flicks its tongue in and out. Suddenly it can smell the frog!

Snakes pick up smells from the air with their tongues. A snake flicking its tongue is like you sniffing with your nose!

That frog must get away fast!

jaws unhook here

elastic muscle
that can stretch
wide open

Snakes do not chew their food. They
swallow it whole by "unhooking"
their jaws.

A python can swallow a whole pig in
one bite.

The coral snake rubs its head on a rock.
Rubbing breaks open the old skin.

Slowly, slowly, the snake crawls out.
Snakes shed their skins two or three times
each year.

A new skin is all grown underneath.
The old skin is worn out. The old skin
peels off. It comes off inside out, like
a T-shirt pulled over your head.

Snakes protect themselves in many ways.
A rattlesnake rattles its tail to make a
loud warning: *Ch-ch-ch-ch-ch!*

The boa curls up into a ball. An enemy can bite its tail. But the boa's head is still safe.

A cottonmouth opens its mouth very, very wide. Enemies flee from the scary sight.

An angry cobra scares away enemies too. It rears up high. It makes its neck big and flat. It jabs forward and gives a loud, sharp *hiss!*

People are often scared of snakes.
And yet snakes help people. They kill
rats and mice that eat crops.

And snake poison is used for medicine.
Experts "milk" the fangs to get out
the drops.

People may fear snakes—or they may like them.

But one thing is certain. Snakes have been around for millions and millions and millions of years.

Way before people, there were snakes. Even back in the time of dinosaurs there were snakes.

Snakes are here to stay!

About the Author

Patricia Demuth

Patricia Demuth loved being outdoors when she was a child. She remembers having "time to explore" with her eight brothers and sisters. She still has "great fun" exploring nature and writing about what she finds.

Snake Problem

by Shel Silverstein

It's not that I don't care for snakes,
But oh what do you do
When a 24-foot python says . . .

Reader Response

Let's Talk

What are three surprising things you learned about snakes?

Think About It

1. Do you think the author finds snakes interesting? Why?

2. How are all snakes alike? How are they different?

3. How do snakes protect themselves?

Write a Snake Poem

Think about what you learned about snakes. Write a poem about a snake. Tell it to a friend.

Spiders Up Close

by Judy Nayer

jumping spider

spider crab

marbled orb weaver

Have You Heard?
There are 30,000 different kinds of spiders!

The world is full of spiders. Spiders have been on Earth since before the first dinosaurs.

burrowing wolf spider

grass spider

water spider

You can find spiders in almost every place! They live on the ground, in trees, and under rocks. They live in sand and in water. They live in people's gardens, and even in people's houses!

Have You Heard?

Spiders can help us because they eat insects that harm our gardens.

Spiders' bodies range in size. Some are as small as the period at the end of this sentence. Some are large enough to cover this page!

tarantula

This jumping spider is so small it fits on a dime.

Have You Heard?

The biggest spider is huge—big enough to eat a mouse!

The female black widow (left) is much larger than the male (right).

The lynx spider is not an insect.

Some people call a spider an insect. But spiders are not insects. Can you tell the difference? Notice that the spider has eight legs. Insects have only six legs. Do not call a spider an insect!

The assassin bug (top) and the June bug (bottom) are insects.

Have You Heard?

Spiders use the hairs on their legs to sense what is around them.

A crab spider's body has two main parts.

1

2

How else can you tell the difference between a spider and an insect? Take a close look. A spider's body has two main parts. An insect's body has three main parts.

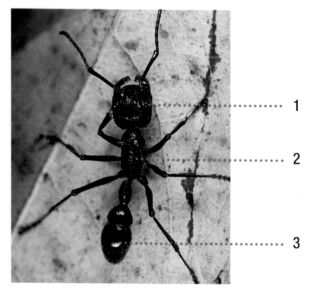

1

2

3

An ant's body has three main parts.

Have You Heard?

Many insects have wings.
Spiders never do.

Some spiders trap insects in a web. A spider's web is made of silk that comes from the spider's own body. Once a spider spins a web, it waits until an insect lands in the web.

This spider moves its web as a warning signal.

A grass spider sits on a wet web.

The orb spider spins a beautiful web.

Some spiders hunt insects the way cats hunt mice. They chase after insects until they can pounce on them.

A wolf spider attacks a cricket.

Have You Heard?

A jumping spider can make a leap forty times longer than its body.

A jumping spider begins its leap.

spider in a funnel web   lynx spider   arrow-shaped spider

golden web spider   trapdoor spider   black widow spider

The world is full of spiders. The
next time you see one, take a close
look. What you see may surprise you.

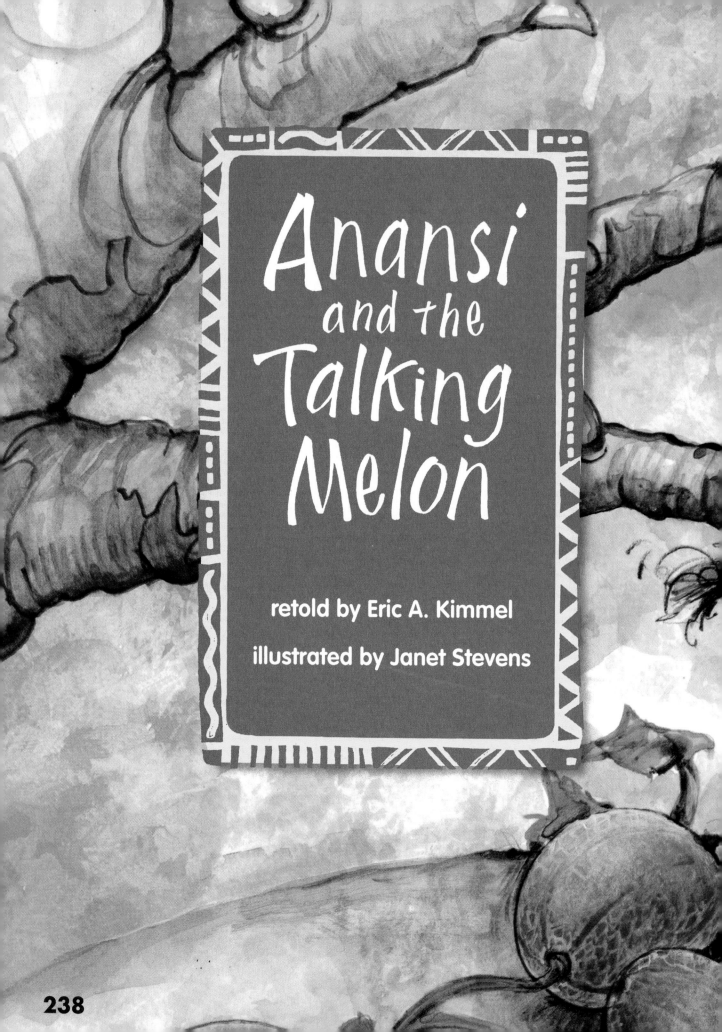

Anansi
and the
Talking
Melon

retold by Eric A. Kimmel

illustrated by Janet Stevens

One fine morning Anansi the Spider sat high up in a thorn tree looking down into Elephant's garden. Elephant was hoeing his melon patch. The ripe melons seemed to call out to Anansi, "Look how juicy and sweet we are! Come eat us!"

Anansi loved to eat melons, but he was much too lazy to grow them himself. So he sat up in the thorn tree, watching and waiting, while the sun rose high in the sky and the day grew warm. By the time noon came, it was too hot to work. Elephant put down his hoe and went inside his house to take a nap.

Here was the moment Anansi had been waiting for. He broke off a thorn and dropped down into the melon patch. He used the thorn to bore a hole in the biggest, ripest melon.

241

Anansi squeezed inside and started eating. He ate and ate until he was as round as a berry.

"I'm full," Anansi said at last. "Elephant will be coming back soon. It is time to go."

But when he tried to squeeze through the
hole, Anansi had a surprise. He didn't fit!
The hole was big enough for a thin spider,
but much too small for a fat one.

"I'm stuck!" Anansi cried. "I can't get out.
I will have to wait until I am thin again."

Anansi sat down
on a pile of melon
seeds and waited
to get thin. Time
passed slowly.

"I'm bored,"
Anansi said. "I wish
I had something to do."

Just then he heard Elephant returning to the garden. Anansi had an idea. "When Elephant gets closer, I will say something. Elephant will think the melon is talking. What fun!"

Elephant walked over to the melon patch.
"Look at this fine melon. How big and ripe it
is!" he said, picking it up.

"Ouch!" cried Anansi.
Elephant jumped.
"Aah! Who said that?"

"I did. The melon," Anansi said.

"I didn't know melons could talk," said Elephant.

"Of course we do. We talk all the time. The trouble is, you never listen."

"I can't believe my ears!" Elephant exclaimed. "A talking melon! Who could believe it? I must show this to the king."

Elephant ran down the road, carrying the melon with Anansi inside. Along the way, he ran into Hippo.

"Where are you going with that melon?" Hippo asked.

"I'm taking it to the king," Elephant told him.

"What for? The king has hundreds of melons."

"He doesn't have one like this," Elephant said. "This is a talking melon."

Hippo didn't believe Elephant. "A talking melon? What an idea! That's as ridiculous as . . ."

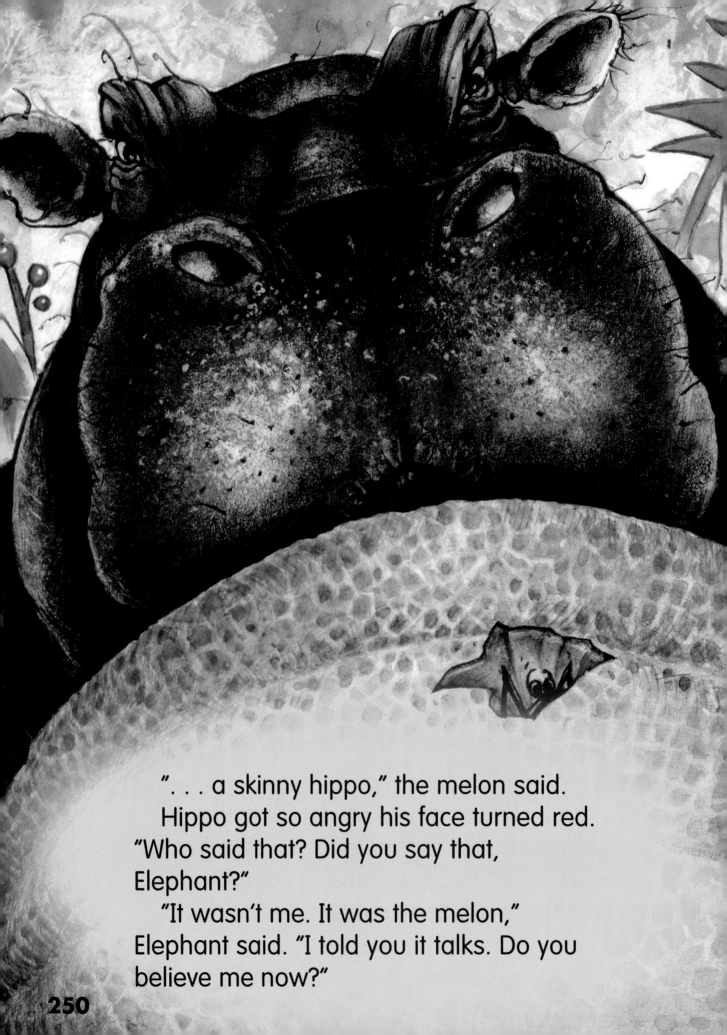

". . . a skinny hippo," the melon said.

Hippo got so angry his face turned red.
"Who said that? Did you say that,
Elephant?"

"It wasn't me. It was the melon,"
Elephant said. "I told you it talks. Do you
believe me now?"

"I do!" Hippo exclaimed. "I want to go with you. I want to hear what the king says when you show him this talking melon."

"Come along, then," said Elephant. So Elephant and Hippo went down the road together, carrying the melon.

By and by, they ran into Warthog. "Where
are you taking that melon?" Warthog asked
them.

"We're taking it to the king," Elephant and
Hippo told him.

"What for? The king has hundreds of melons," Warthog said.

"He doesn't have one like this," Hippo replied. "This melon talks. I heard it."

Warthog started to laugh. "A talking melon? Why, that's as ridiculous as . . ."

". . . a handsome warthog," said the melon.
Warthog got so angry he shook all over.
"Who said that? Did you say that, Elephant?
Did you say that, Hippo?"

"Of course not!" Hippo and Elephant told
him. "The melon talks. Do you believe us now?"

"I do!" cried Warthog. "Let me go with you. I want to see what the king does when you show him this talking melon."

So Warthog, Elephant, and Hippo went down the road together, carrying the melon.

Along the way, they met Ostrich, Rhino, and Turtle. They didn't believe the melon could talk either until they heard it for themselves. Then they wanted to come along too.

The animals came before the king.
Elephant bowed low as he placed the melon
at the king's feet.

The king looked down. "Why did you bring
me a melon?" he asked Elephant. "I have
hundreds of melons growing in my garden."

"You don't have one like this," Elephant
said. "This melon talks."

"A talking melon? I don't believe it. Say
something, Melon." The king prodded the
melon with his foot.

The melon said nothing.

"Melon," the king said in a slightly louder
voice, "there is no reason to be shy. Say
whatever you like. I only want to hear you talk."

The melon still said nothing. The king grew impatient.

"Melon, if you can talk, I want you to say something. I command you to speak."

The melon did not make a sound.
The king gave up. "Oh, this is a stupid melon!" he said.

Just then the melon spoke. "Stupid, am I? Why do you say that? I'm not the one who talks to melons!"

The animals had never seen the king so angry. "How dare this melon insult me!" he shouted. The king picked up the melon and hurled it as far as he could.

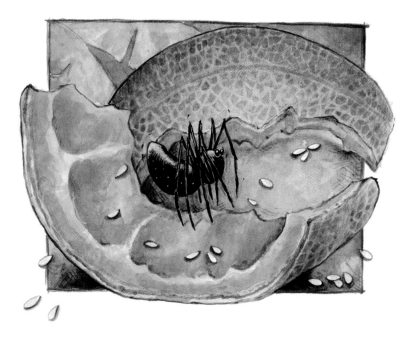

The melon bounced and rolled all the way to Elephant's house. *KPOM!* It smacked into the thorn tree and burst into pieces. Anansi picked himself up from among the bits of melon rind.

All the excitement had made him thin. And now that he was thin again, he was hungry. Anansi climbed the banana tree. He settled himself in the middle of a big bunch of bananas and started eating.

Elephant returned. He went straight to the melon patch.

"You melons got me in trouble with the king!" Elephant said. "From now on, you can talk all you like. I'm not going to listen to a word you say!"

"Good for you, Elephant!" Anansi called from the bananas. "We bananas should have warned you. Talking melons are nothing but trouble."

About the Author and the Illustrator

Eric A. Kimmel

Eric A. Kimmel is an author and a storyteller. He likes telling folktales. Mr. Kimmel likes stories that are fun and can teach something. "Kids are an excellent audience," he says.

Janet Stevens

"I have been drawing as long as I can remember," says Janet Stevens. Her family called her "the artist" when she was a child.

The animals she draws often wear sneakers and Hawaiian shirts!

Let's Talk

Would it be fun to be Anansi?

Think About It

1. What makes this story funny?

2. What do you think the animals might say about the talking melon after the story ends?

3. Suppose that the story kept going. What do you think might happen next?

Be a Mime

Act out your favorite part of the story without using any words. Then have someone read that part as you act it out.

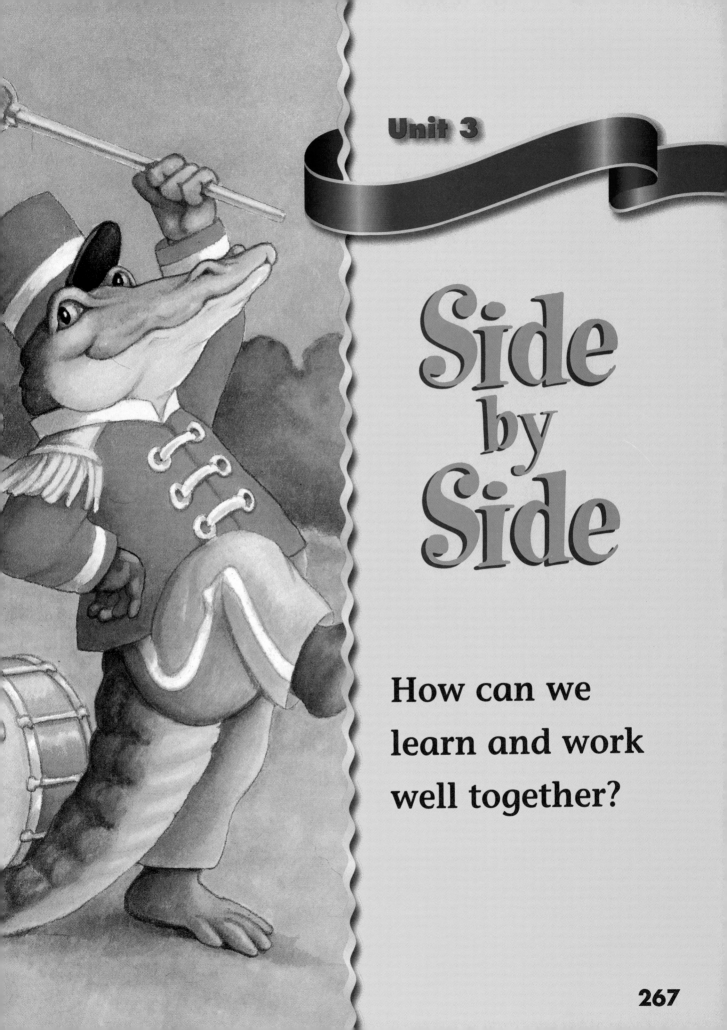

Side by Side

How can we learn and work well together?

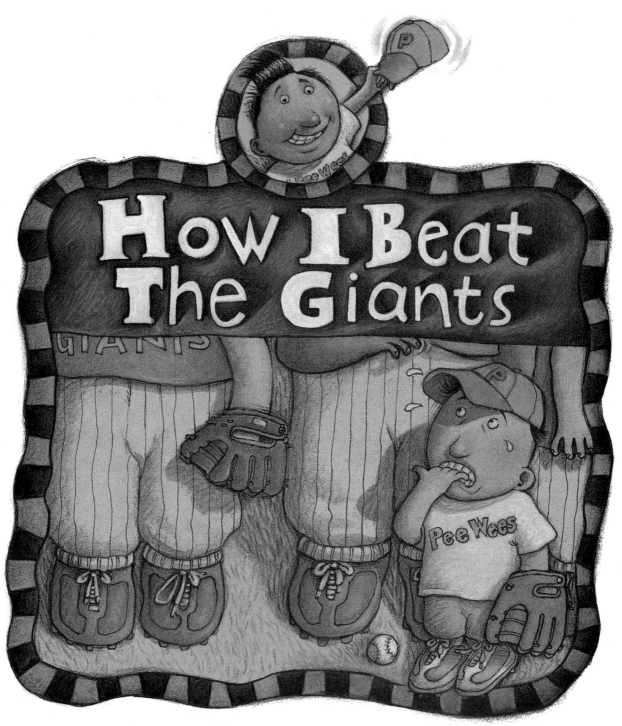

by Anne Phillips
illustrated by Jack Davis

My friends and I had a game against
the Giants. It turned out they really were
giants! Those players were as big as
trees.

"Don't worry," said Howie.
"We'll show those giants."
But after the Giants batted,
the score was a hundred to zero.
Things were beginning to look bad.

269

Now it was my turn at bat. I gripped
the bat and swung. Strike one! Strike
two! Strike three! I was out! Things were
getting worse.

Jamie's been our best batter since first grade. She hit the ball. She ran around the bases. It was a run! The Giants were still winning, but things were getting better.

A little later, the Giants had a
thousand. We had a thousand and one.
The Giants were batting. Now, if we
could get them out, we could win the
game.

"Watch out!" said Kim. I nodded.
I pitched the ball. *Crack!* The ball flew
through the clouds all the way to the
moon. Then it bounced back! Wow!

"I've got it!" I shouted. I caught the
ball. Jamie caught me. Howie caught
Jamie. Kim caught Howie.

The Giants were out! We had won!

So that's how I beat the Giants. . .
with a little help from my friends.

Play Ball

by Stephen Krensky

illustrated by Susanna Natti

Lionel and his friends were playing baseball.
Lionel was getting a lot of advice.

"Dive for those balls, Lionel,"
said Jeffrey, when a ball got past him.

"Catch with two hands," said Sarah,
when a ball jumped off his glove.

When Lionel came up to bat, Ellen
was pitching.
"Easy out," she said.

Lionel gripped the bat firmly.

He would show her how wrong she was.

Ellen made her windup.

The pitch sailed in.

Lionel waited—and then he swung hard.

The bat met the ball

with a sharp *Craaccck!*

The ball went up and up and up.

It sailed over a fence.

CRASH!

"That sounded like a window," said Max.

"At the Barries'," said Sarah.

Lionel froze. He squeezed his eyes shut.
This was going to be terrible.
Mr. Barrie was bound to yell at him.

His parents would find out.
They would yell too.

Lionel opened his eyes. Mr. Barrie
was approaching with a ball
in his hand.

"Who hit this ball?" he asked.
Lionel swallowed hard.

He didn't want anyone else
getting in trouble for his mistake.
"I did," he said.

"I hit it too," said Jeffrey behind him.
He had picked up his bat.

"And me," said Max,
his bat now resting on his shoulder.

"I got a piece of it," said George.

"Don't forget me," said Sarah.

"And us," said everyone else together.
They were all holding their bats.

Mr. Barrie looked around.
"I see," he said, trying to look serious.

"It was a real team effort."
He rubbed his chin.

"Well, since you all shared in the hit,
you can all help me fix the window later.
Fair enough?"

Everyone nodded.

Mr. Barrie returned to his house.

Lionel looked at everybody and sighed.
"Thanks," he said.

Jeffrey smiled. "It could have been any of us.
Besides," he added, "that's what friends are for."

Stephen Krensky

Stephen Krensky says that when he writes for children, he writes "the kind of stories I like best." He has many interests. He writes about them in his books. He has written about ice cream, dinosaurs, treasure hunts, and trolls. He dedicated "Play Ball" to "all the friends on Eaton Road." That's where Mr. Krensky lives.

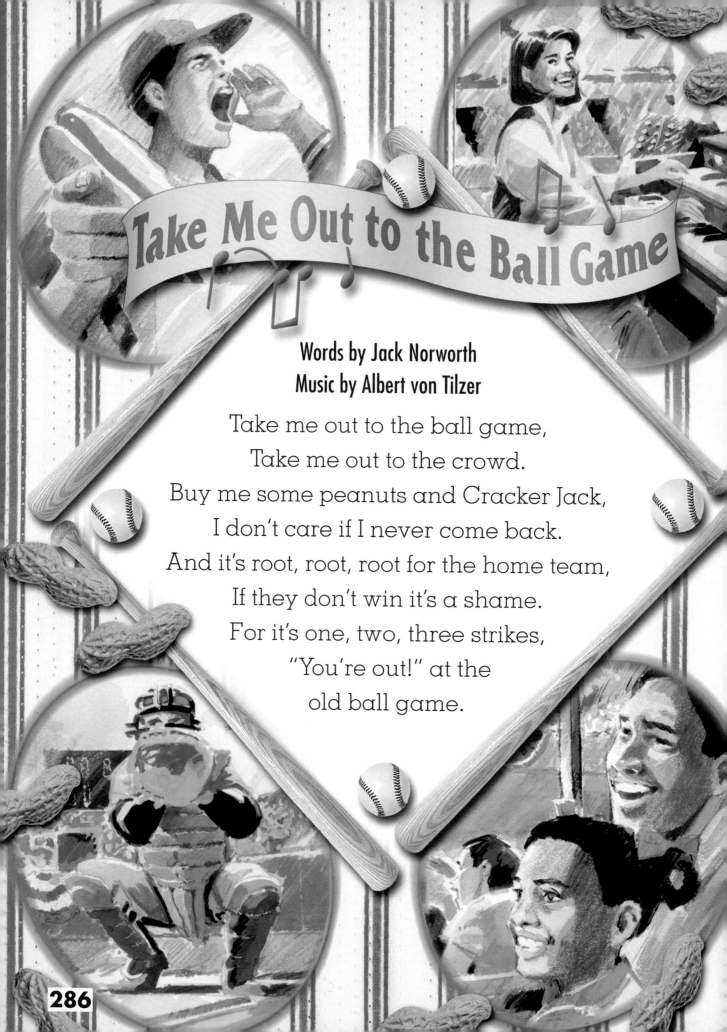

Take Me Out to the Ball Game

Words by Jack Norworth
Music by Albert von Tilzer

Take me out to the ball game,
Take me out to the crowd.
Buy me some peanuts and Cracker Jack,
I don't care if I never come back.
And it's root, root, root for the home team,
If they don't win it's a shame.
For it's one, two, three strikes,
"You're out!" at the
old ball game.

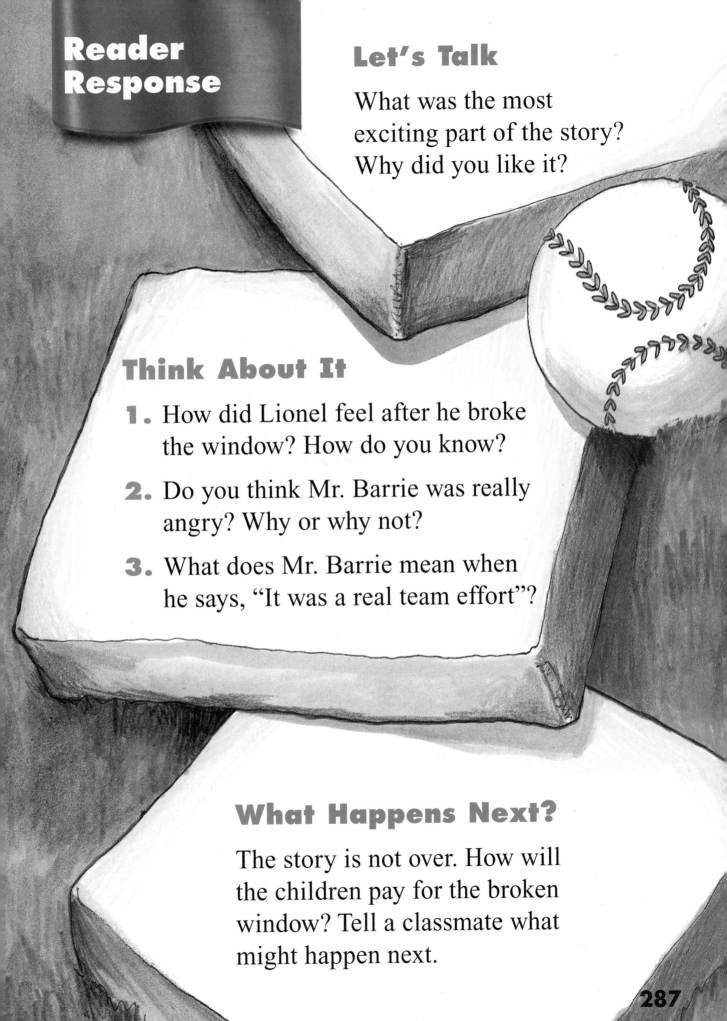

Let's Talk

What was the most exciting part of the story? Why did you like it?

Think About It

1. How did Lionel feel after he broke the window? How do you know?

2. Do you think Mr. Barrie was really angry? Why or why not?

3. What does Mr. Barrie mean when he says, "It was a real team effort"?

What Happens Next?

The story is not over. How will the children pay for the broken window? Tell a classmate what might happen next.

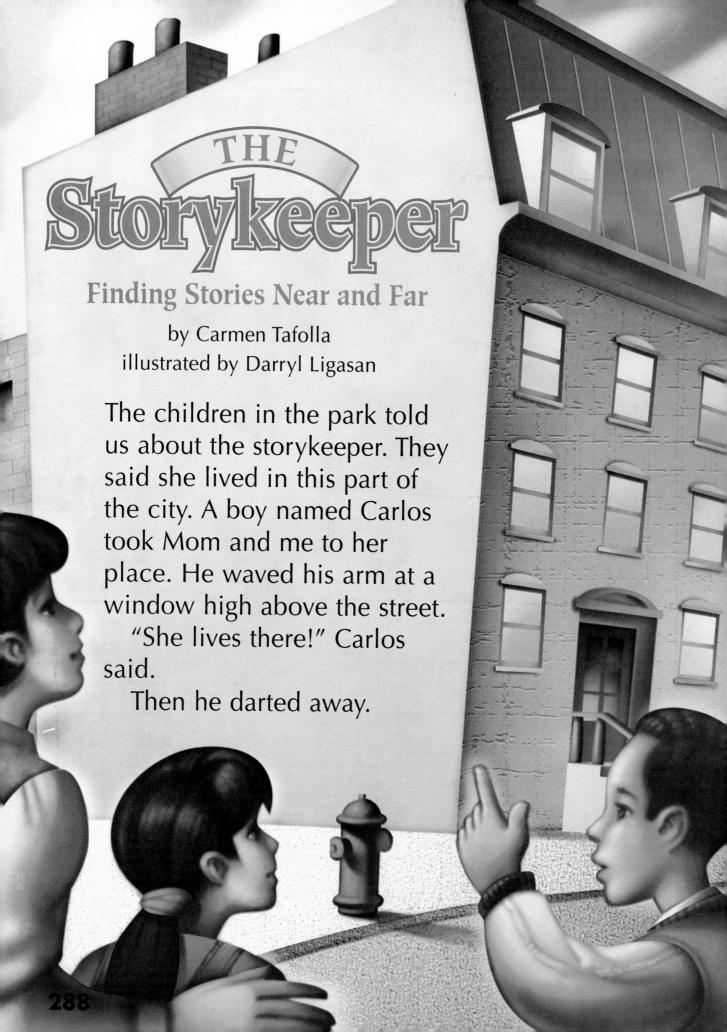

THE Storykeeper

Finding Stories Near and Far

by Carmen Tafolla

illustrated by Darryl Ligasan

The children in the park told us about the storykeeper. They said she lived in this part of the city. A boy named Carlos took Mom and me to her place. He waved his arm at a window high above the street.

"She lives there!" Carlos said.

Then he darted away.

The storykeeper has dark hair and eyes as bright as stars. I liked her as soon as I met her. We sat in a large room. Here are my questions and her answers.

Q: Are you the storykeeper?

A: Yes! That is what the children call me.

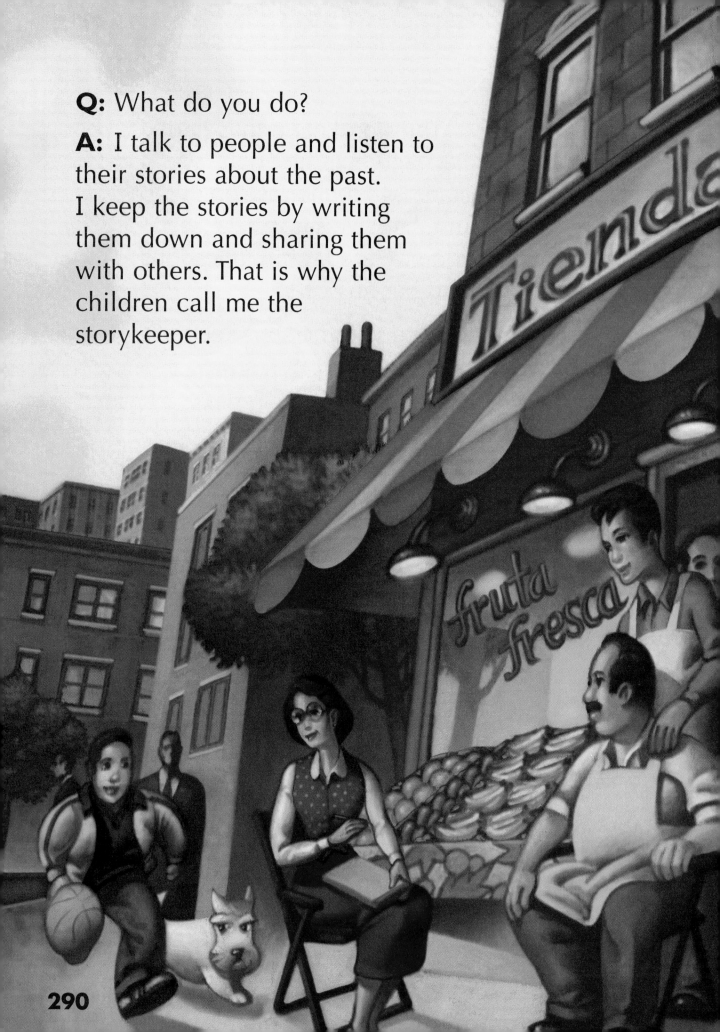

Q: What do you do?

A: I talk to people and listen to their stories about the past. I keep the stories by writing them down and sharing them with others. That is why the children call me the storykeeper.

Q: Where do you find these stories?

A: It's not hard. I find stories every place I go. A story can be hiding in a dark room of a house or high in an old barn. Once a paper in a large jar led me to a story.

Q: Do you ever go far to find a story?

A: Sometimes I go to a city far away. I go many places to find stories. But most of the time I start here. In this city there are many stories.

Once I met a man with a guitar in the park. He told stories with his songs.

292

Q: Why are these stories so important?

A: I'm hoping that if we learn stories about each other, we can start to make the world a better place.

"Thank you," I said. "I can hardly wait to tell other children what you have shared with me."

"Good!" she said. "Then you will be a storykeeper too!"

People, People, Everywhere!

by Nancy Van Laan

illustrated by Nadine Bernard Westcott

People, people, everywhere!
Running here, running there!
People racing round the town,
Going up!
Going down!
People riding to the top.
Getting off!
Please press *STOP!*

People dashing round the park,
Walking dogs . . .
Bark! Bark! Bark!

People waiting in a line.
Here's the bus!
Just in time!

Catching taxis . . . catching trains . . .
Catching subways . . . catching planes.
Take a copter
Up! Up! Up!
Take a ferry,
Shlup! Shlup! Shlup!

People, people, everywhere!
Working here, working there.
Policemen walking city beats.
Vendors selling treats to eat.

SHOP

BREAD

Workers building buildings tall,
Way up high.
Watch out! Don't fall!

People working under town,
Digging, fixing, underground.
Tunneling subways, sealing leaks,
Way beneath the city streets.

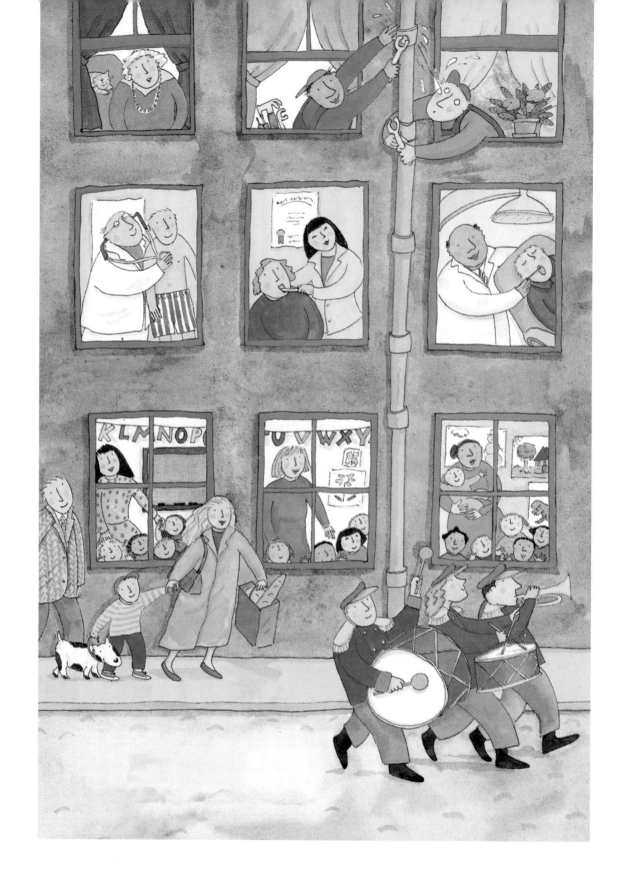

Teachers teaching . . . plumbers plumbing . . .
Doctors doctoring . . . drummers drumming . . .

Here's a fire truck
Whizzing, wailing!
In the harbor,
Boats are sailing!

Children, children, everywhere!
Playing here, playing there.
In the alleys . . . at the park . . .
In the hallways after dark.
Jumping rope, playing ball,
Playing anything at all!
Riding bikes, tic-tac-toe,
Children shouting, "Go! Go! Go!"
Upstairs, downstairs,
Running round,
Children playing all through town!

People, people, everywhere!
Leaving here, going there.
Moving to a quiet place
In the country where there's space.
Room to work and room to play,
No more waiting every day.
No more traffic, no more noise,
Lots of space for lots of toys.

Trees and flowers all around,
A perfect place to build a town.

People here, people there,
People, people, everywhere!

FUTURE SITE OF TOWN PARK

FOR SALE

SAVE OUR EARTH

RECYCLE

TRASH

About the Author
Nancy Van Laan

Nancy Van Laan has always liked to write. "When I was little, I would spend long afternoons writing poems, plays, and stories," she says.

Ms. Van Laan writes her stories by hand. "My pages are full of scribbles and cross-outs."

About the Illustrator
Nadine Bernard Westcott

Nadine Bernard Westcott first planned to become a teacher. Instead she became a very popular book illustrator.

Ms. Westcott remembers drawing as a child. She sketched on the back of paper place mats.

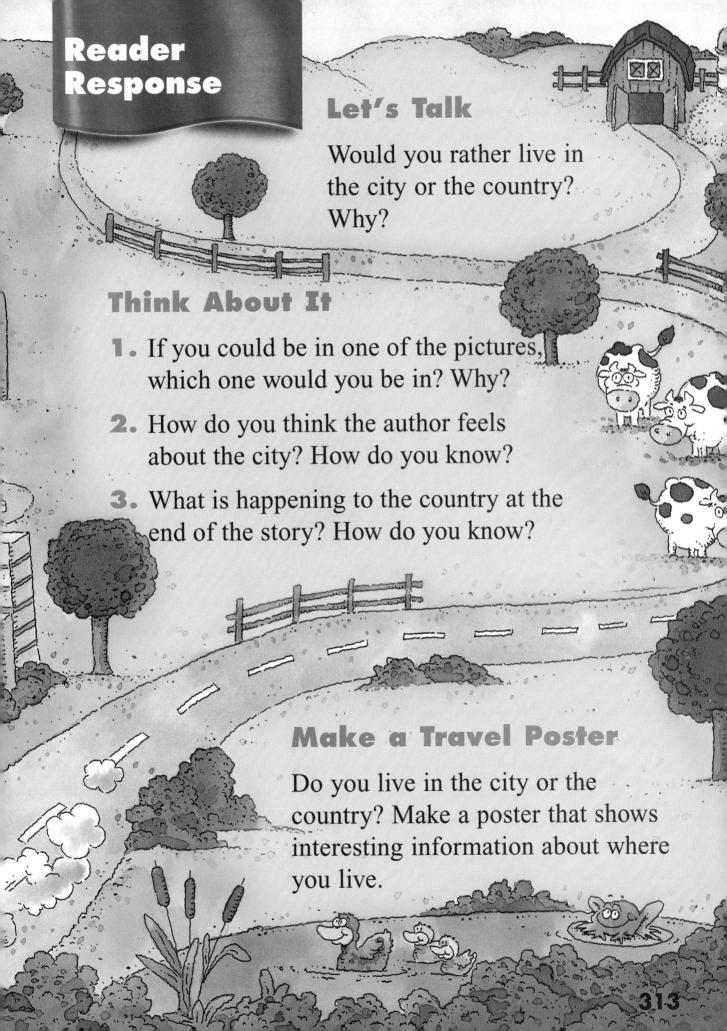

Reader Response

Let's Talk

Would you rather live in the city or the country? Why?

Think About It

1. If you could be in one of the pictures, which one would you be in? Why?

2. How do you think the author feels about the city? How do you know?

3. What is happening to the country at the end of the story? How do you know?

Make a Travel Poster

Do you live in the city or the country? Make a poster that shows interesting information about where you live.

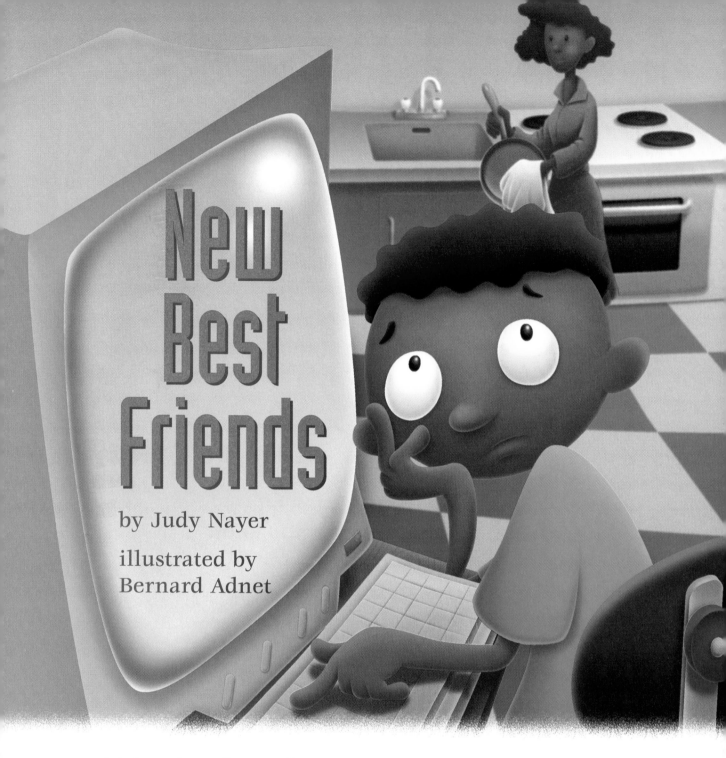

New Best Friends

by Judy Nayer

illustrated by
Bernard Adnet

Hal missed Uncle Lou. His uncle flew
home a few weeks ago.

"Why don't you write Uncle Lou a letter?"
said his mom. "He'd love to hear from you."

So Hal did. He used his computer.

Dear Uncle Lou,

How are you? What's new? There's a new boy in my school. He's really cool. He likes computers as much as I do.

Love,
Hal

P.S. Write back soon.

A few days later,
Hal wrote to Uncle
Lou again.

Dear Uncle Lou,
    You're not going to believe
it! The new boy lives across
the street! We sometimes
walk to school together.
                    Love,
                    Hal
P.S. His name is Luís!

Hal wrote to
Uncle Lou again.

Dear Uncle Lou,
   Luís likes basketball too!
Today we played in his driveway.
   Luís ran toward me and threw
the ball. I took my best shot, but
the ball didn't go in. Then it was
his turn. He threw the ball with
one hand. It flew right through
the hoop!

                    Love,
                    Hal

P.S. Are you coming again soon?

Hal didn't write to Uncle Lou for a few days because he was too busy playing with Luís. They either played computer games or basketball. Sometimes they wrote stories on their computers.

Then Hal wrote Uncle Lou again.

Dear Uncle Lou,

You've got to see the room Luís has. We either play with his computer or with his other cool space stuff. We even learned about the crew that flew to the moon. Zoom! Zoom!

Love,

Hal

P.S. Luís says I'm his best friend. Isn't that cool?

The next day Hal got a letter from Uncle Lou. Hal read it on his computer.

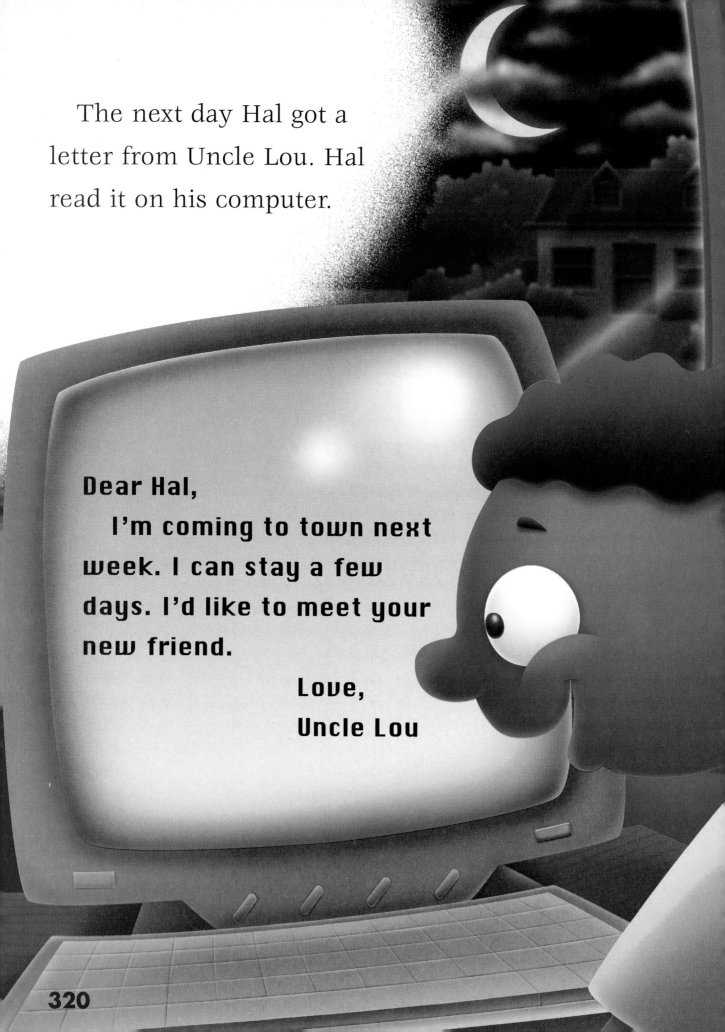

Dear Hal,

I'm coming to town next week. I can stay a few days. I'd like to meet your new friend.

Love,
Uncle Lou

Uncle Lou arrived on Tuesday afternoon.

He and Hal's new best friend, Luís, got along just fine.

WANTED: BEST FRIEND

by A. M. Monson
illustrated by Lynn Munsinger

Cat and Mouse sat at the table. They were playing checkers. The two played the game so often that Cat sometimes made up new rules.

"That's it," said Cat. "I won." He set up the checkers for another game.

"That's the third time you've won,"
complained Mouse. "Let's play crazy eights now."

"I hate crazy eights," said Cat. "You take
forever to decide which card to play."

"But when we play crazy eights, I win
sometimes," said Mouse. He folded his arms
across his chest. "Either we play crazy eights
or I go home."

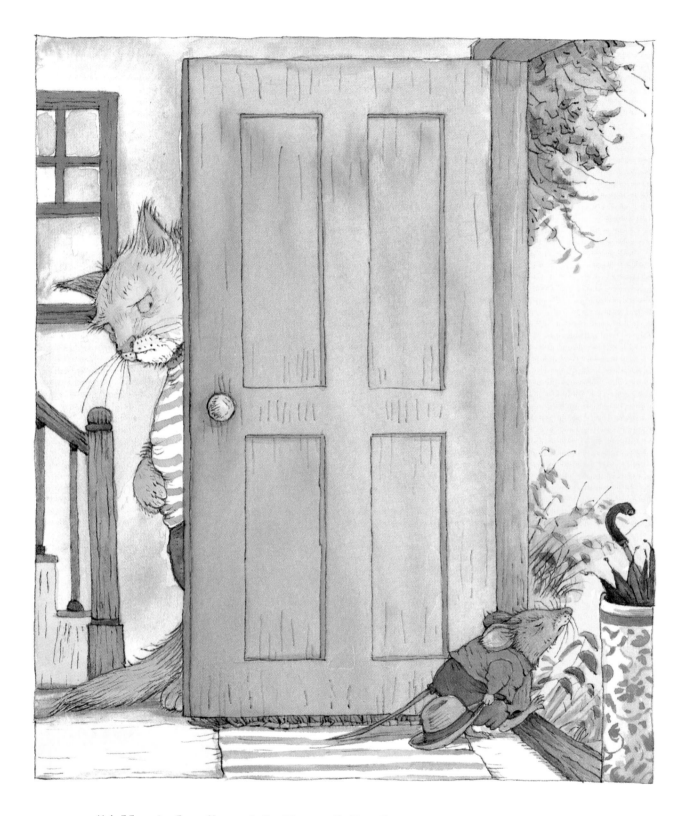

"All right," said Cat. "Go home. I'll find
someone else to play with me."

"Fine," said Mouse. He picked up his hat
and left.

Cat scratched his head. How would he find
another friend? Suddenly he had an idea.
He grabbed a piece of paper and a pencil.
He wrote:

WANTED: BEST FRIEND
MUST LIKE TO PLAY GAMES
SEE CAT *IMMEDIATELY!*

Then he called *The Hollow Log Gazette.*

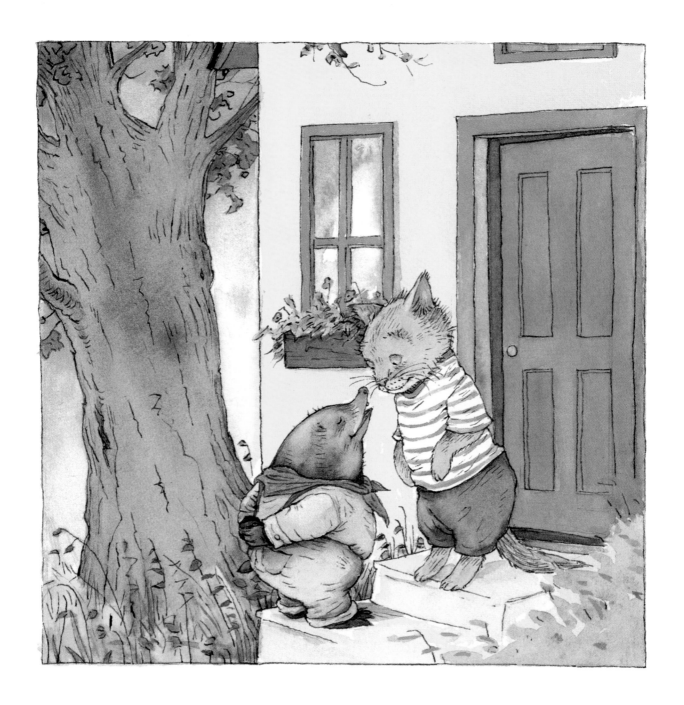

Two days later there was a knock at Cat's door.
"Did you advertise for a friend?" asked Mole.
"Yes," answered Cat. "Come in." He hoped Mole
liked to play checkers as much as he did.

"How about some munchies?" asked Mole.

"Help yourself," said Cat.

Mole disappeared into the kitchen.

When he came out, he was carrying a can of soda, a jar of peanut butter, crackers, bananas, an ice cream bar, and a bag of pretzels. The can of soda tumbled to the floor. Mole kicked it toward the table.

"Ah-h," said Mole. He tossed the banana peel over his shoulder. "Now I'm ready to play."

Cat moved his checker first. Mole stuffed his mouth with crackers and peanut butter.

"Your turn," said Cat.

Mole dumped all the pretzels onto the table, then moved his playing piece.

Cat smiled. He jumped over Mole's checker using his own. "Oh, dear," said Cat. His finger sank into a gooey glob of peanut butter when he touched Mole's checker.

"Time for a drink," said Mole. "No, wait!" said Cat. But he was too late. Orange soda sprayed from the can into Cat's face.

"This will not do," said Cat. He raced for a towel. "You cannot be a slob and be my best friend."

Cat avoided Mole's sticky fingers and led him by the arm out of the house.

He'd just finished cleaning up Mole's mess
when he heard another knock at the door.

"Did you advertise for a friend?" asked Otter.
He carried a large and bumpy duffel bag.
"Yes, I did," said Cat. "Come in."

"I have everything we need to have fun," said Otter. He unzipped the bag. "Baseball, basketball, softball, football, soccer ball . . ."

"But I like to play checkers," said Cat. Balls bounced around his feet.

"B-or-ring!" said Otter. "These games are a lot more fun. Watch." He grabbed the basketball and tossed it into a lamp shade.

"Two points!" he yelled.

Cat raced to steady the wobbling lamp.
A football sailed past his head and through
the rabbit ears on the television.

"Touchdown!" cheered Otter.

"No more," said Cat. But he was too late.
Otter kicked the soccer ball into the fireplace.

"Goal!" cried Otter.

"This will not do," said Cat.
He stamped out sparks. "You cannot burn my house down and be my best friend."

He made Otter pick up all the balls, then showed him to the door.

He plopped into his big stuffed chair. "If Mouse had a phone, I would call and invite him back." Suddenly he had an idea. He grabbed a piece of paper and a pencil. He wrote:

MOUSE,
PLEASE COME BACK.
WILLING TO PLAY CRAZY EIGHTS.
CAT

Then he called *The Hollow Log Gazette*.
Two days later there was a knock at Cat's door.

"Mouse," said Cat. "I'm so happy to see you."
He led his friend to the table.

"I'm thirsty," said Mouse. He disappeared into
the kitchen, then returned with a glass of water.

Cat watched Mouse set the glass on a napkin. "You're so tidy," said Cat.

"Thank you," said Mouse.

"And you never throw things around my house," said Cat.

"I wouldn't dream of it," said Mouse.

Cat smiled. "Mouse," he said, "you're *my* kind of best friend."

And the two of them began to play crazy eights.

About the Author and the Illustrator

A. M. Monson

A. M. Monson went to a one-room school in Wisconsin. She is an animal lover and enjoys nature.

Ms. Monson now lives in Minnesota. She likes to cross-country ski and camp.

Lynn Munsinger

Lynn Munsinger is the illustrator of over forty children's books. She is well known for her drawings of Tacky the Penguin.

Ms. Munsinger lives in New York City with her two dogs. She likes to ski and travel.

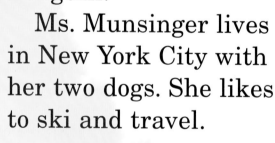

Reader Response

Let's Talk

Would you want Cat for a friend? Why or why not?

Think About It

1. How does Cat feel about Mouse at the beginning of the story?

2. Why does Cat decide to play crazy eights with Mouse at the end of the story?

3. Why does Mouse forgive Cat?

Place a Want Ad

You are Cat. Write a new want ad. Write three things that tell what you really want in a friend.

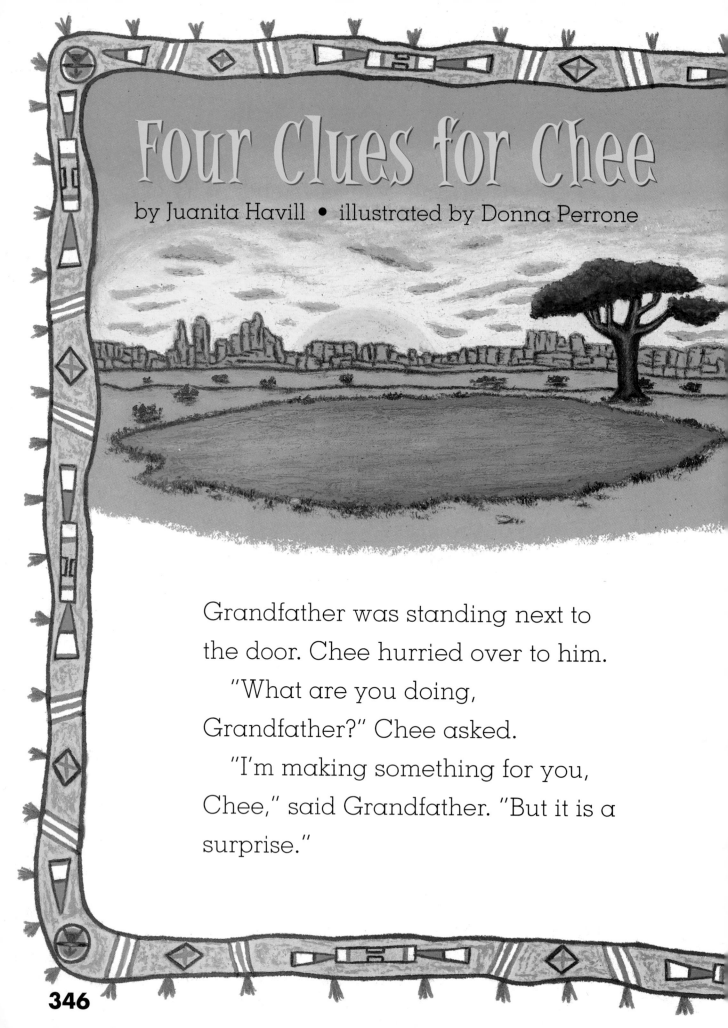

Four Clues for Chee

by Juanita Havill • illustrated by Donna Perrone

Grandfather was standing next to
the door. Chee hurried over to him.

"What are you doing,
Grandfather?" Chee asked.

"I'm making something for you,
Chee," said Grandfather. "But it is a
surprise."

Then Grandfather said, "I will give you four clues. My surprise comes from a tree. There is nothing in it, but something pours out of it. It can sound like a bird or an echo in a canyon."

Next, he gave Chee one more clue. "Breath and fingers bring its sound to us."

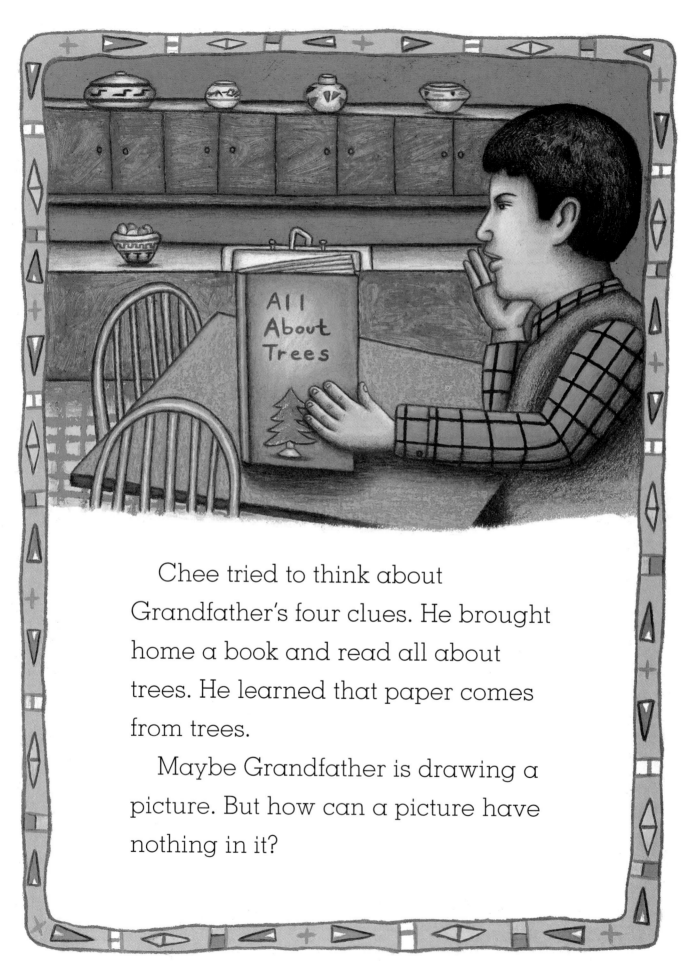

Chee tried to think about Grandfather's four clues. He brought home a book and read all about trees. He learned that paper comes from trees.

Maybe Grandfather is drawing a picture. But how can a picture have nothing in it?

Chee's mother brought food home from the store. Chee carried the boxes to the kitchen for her. A box can be empty, he thought. A box can come from a tree.

Next, Chee thought about the third clue. A box can't sound like a bird. He tried shouting in the box. A box doesn't sound like a bird or a canyon.

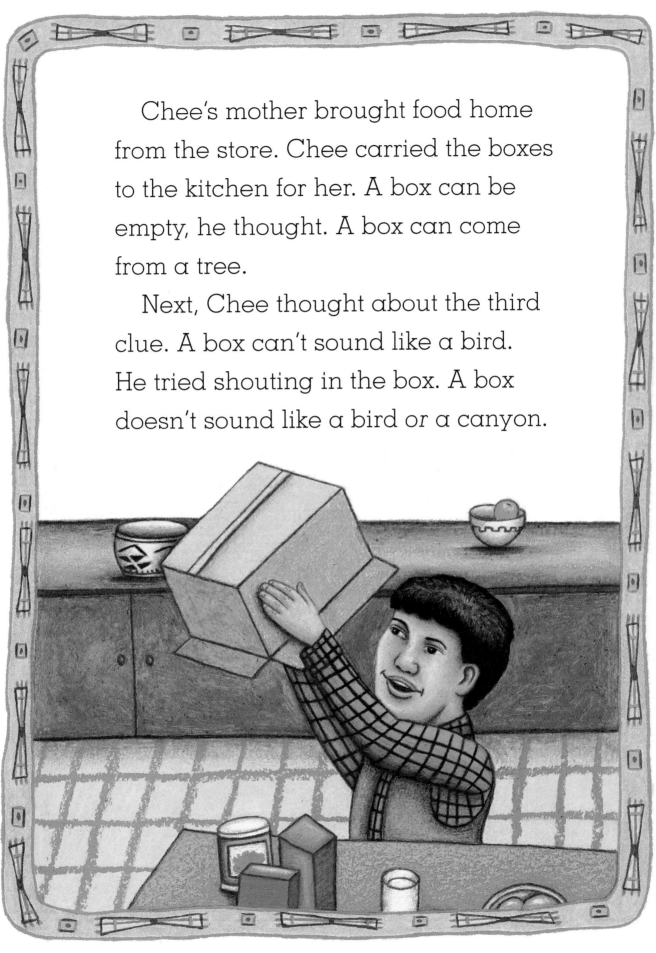

Chee cried out his name to the canyon. "Chee! Chee! Chee!" the canyon sang. Then he knew.

"With your gift I will make sounds," Chee said to Grandfather. "I will use my breath and my fingers."

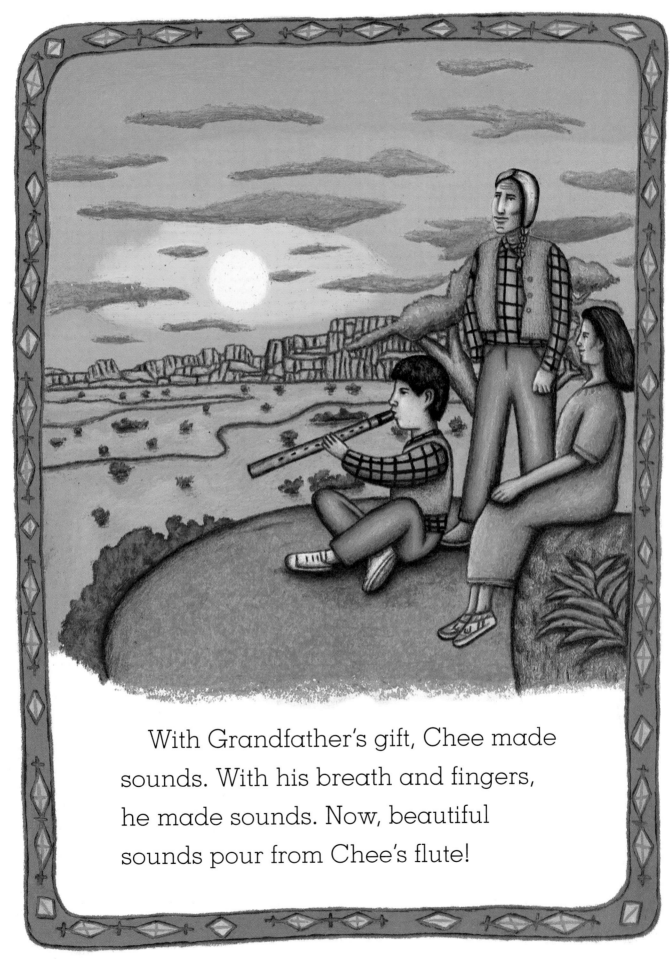

With Grandfather's gift, Chee made
sounds. With his breath and fingers,
he made sounds. Now, beautiful
sounds pour from Chee's flute!

Young Cam Jansen
and the Dinosaur Game

by David A. Adler

illustrated by Susanna Natti

CONTENTS

1. I'm Going! I'm Going!

Honk! Honk!

"I'm going! I'm going!" Mr. Jansen said. He was driving his daughter Cam and her friend Eric Shelton to a birthday party.

Mr. Jansen stopped at the corner. He looked at the street signs. Then he said, "I'm sorry. I forgot where the party is. And I forgot to bring the invitation."

Honk! Honk!

"I'm going! I'm going!" Mr. Jansen said as he drove on. "But I don't know *where* I'm going."

Mr. Jansen drove to the next corner and parked the car.

Eric said, "I'm sure Cam remembers where the party is."

Cam closed her eyes and said, "Click!" Cam always closes her eyes and says "Click!" when she wants to remember something.

Cam has an amazing memory. "My memory is like a camera," she says. "I have a picture in my head of everything I've seen. 'Click!' is the sound my camera makes."

Cam's real name is Jennifer. But because of her great memory, people started to call her "the Camera." Then "the Camera" became just Cam.

"I'm looking at the invitation," Cam said, with her eyes closed. "It says, 'Come to a party for Jane Bell. 3:00 P.M., 86 Robin Lane.'"

Cam opened her eyes.

Mr. Jansen drove to 86 Robin Lane. There were balloons and a big HAPPY BIRTHDAY sign on the front door.

Mr. Bell opened the door and said, "Come in. Come in." He pointed to a big jar. "Before you join the others, guess how many dinosaurs are in this jar. Remember your guess. The best one wins the dinosaurs."

The jar was filled with blue, green, yellow, and red toy dinosaurs. Next to the jar were slips of paper, a few pens, and a shoe box.

Cam tried to count the dinosaurs. But she couldn't. Lots of dinosaurs were hidden behind other dinosaurs.

Cam wrote her guess on a slip of paper. She put the paper in the shoe box.

Eric looked at the jar. He looked for a long time. Then he wrote his guess on a slip of paper too. He put the paper in the shoe box. Eric said, "I hope I win."

Then Cam and Eric went to the kitchen. Their friends were there, sitting around the table.

2. The Dinosaur Game

Mrs. Bell said, "Good, everyone is here. I'll get the birthday cake." She carried a large cake to the table. The cake was covered with chocolate icing. Mrs. Bell lit the candles. Everyone sang "Happy Birthday." Then Mrs. Bell gave each child a piece of birthday cake.

They were all eating cake when Mr. Bell walked into the room. "I counted the dinosaurs," he said.

"There were 154 in the jar." Mr. Bell took a large piece of birthday cake.

Eric said, "I guessed 150. Maybe I'll win."

Rachel said, "I guessed 300."

"Who won?" Jane asked. "Who won the dinosaur game?"

Mr. Bell smiled. "We'll see," he said, "as soon as I finish eating."

Some children took a second piece of cake. Some went into the den to play.

When Mr. Bell finished, he brought in the shoe box. He turned it over and picked up a slip of paper. "180," he read. Then he showed it to everyone.

"That was my guess," Jane said.

One by one Mr. Bell read the guesses. "100 . . . 300 . . . 1,000 . . . 450 . . . 200."

Cam said, "200 was my guess."

Mr. Bell looked at the next slip of paper. He read, "150."

"That was my guess," Eric said.

Then Mr. Bell held up the last slip of paper and read, "154."

"That's mine," Robert said. "I win."

"You *do* win," Mr. Bell said. "You guessed the exact number. And here's your prize." He gave Robert the jar of dinosaurs.

Cam looked at Robert. Then she looked at the slip of paper in Mr. Bell's hand and said, "Click!"

Eric whispered to Cam, "That's amazing. He guessed the exact number of dinosaurs."

"Yes," Cam said. "It is amazing. It's almost *too* amazing."

3. Click!

Robert spilled the dinosaurs onto the table.

"They're cute," Rachel said.

"Can I have one?" Jason asked.

Rachel asked, "Can I have one too?"

"I'm not giving them away," Robert said. "I'm selling them."

"I want a red one," Rachel said. "I'll give you the money at school tomorrow."

"I want three green dinosaurs and two yellows," Jason said.

Mrs. Bell said, "Let's play another guessing game." She held up a small box. "I have something in here. It has a face and it runs. What is it?"

"Does it run fast?" Rachel asked.

Mrs. Bell said, "I hope not."

Eric asked, "Does it have eight legs? Is it a spider?"

Mrs. Bell said, "It doesn't have any legs."

Cam asked, "Does it have hands? Is it a watch?"

Cam was right.

Mr. Bell said, "Now let's play musical chairs." He set six chairs in a line. He turned on some music.

Then Mr. Bell told the children, "Walk around the chairs. When the music stops, sit down. Whoever can't find a seat is out of the game."

The children walked around the chairs. But not Cam. She looked at the chairs. She counted them. Then she closed her eyes and said, "Click!"

4. You Made Me Lose

The music stopped. Everyone but Cam sat down. She was out of the game. Mr. Bell took one chair away and turned on the music again.

Cam opened her eyes. She went over to the table. She looked at the slips of paper. Then, as Eric walked past, she whispered to him, "I have something to show you."

Eric turned, and the music stopped. Everyone but Eric sat down. He was out of the game. Mr. Bell took one chair away and turned on the music again.

When Robert walked past, Cam whispered to him, "And I have something to show you."

Robert turned, and the music stopped. Everyone but Robert sat down. Robert was out of the game. He told Cam, "You made me lose at musical chairs."

Cam said, "And I'll make you lose the dinosaurs too."

5. I'm Sharing

Cam said to Robert, "You wrote 154 *after* Jane's father counted the dinosaurs."

"I did not!" Robert said.

Cam told him, "Mr. Bell turned over the shoe box. The papers fell out upside down. They fell out in the same order they were put in.

Jane's guess was first. Eric and I were the last to come to the party. Our guesses should have been last. But yours was."

Robert said, "Maybe the papers got mixed up."

Cam told him, "There were eight guesses but only seven kids are at the party. You guessed twice. You guessed when you came to the party. You guessed again after Jane's father told us there were 154 dinosaurs in the jar."

"I did not," Robert said.

Cam picked up Robert's winning guess. "And look at this," she said.

Cam pointed to a chocolate smudge. "You wrote this after we had birthday cake. That's why there's chocolate on it."

Cam and Eric looked at Robert's hands. There was chocolate on them too.

Robert looked down. "You're right," he said softly. "My real guess was 1,000 dinosaurs."

Robert put the dinosaurs back in the jar.

After the game of musical chairs ended, Robert talked to Mrs. Bell. He told her that Eric had really won the dinosaur game.

Mrs. Bell gave the jar to Eric.

Rachel said, "I want to buy a red dinosaur."

Jason said, "I want three green dinosaurs and two yellows."

Eric told them, "I'm not selling the dinosaurs. I'm sharing them."

The children sat in a circle. Eric walked around them. "One for you," he said as he gave each child a dinosaur. "And one for you. And one for you."

After Eric had given everyone else a dinosaur, he put one on an empty chair and said, "And one for me."

Eric walked around the circle again and again. He walked around until the big jar of toy dinosaurs was empty.

About the Author
David A. Adler

David A. Adler always liked to tell stories. When he was young, he made up stories to tell his brothers and sisters. Now Mr. Adler writes for children. "I feel very fortunate. I love writing, and it's so exciting for me to know that children enjoy reading what I have written."

"I have real fun with the Cam Jansen books," Mr. Adler says. "She is a delightful character."

About the Illustrator
Susanna Natti

Susanna Natti loves to read and draw. She likes to visit schools and talk about her artwork. Ms. Natti has illustrated all the Cam Jansen books as well as the Lionel books, written by Stephen Krensky.

Reader Response

Let's Talk

Did the story keep you interested? Why or why not?

Think About It

1. Why does Cam think that someone cheated in the dinosaur game?

2. Why does Eric decide to share his dinosaurs at the end of the story?

3. How do you feel about Robert? Do you like him? Why or why not?

Be a Mystery Writer

Write your own mystery story.
Ask a classmate to solve the mystery.

A Good Laugh for Cookie

by Deborah Eaton
illustrated by
C.D. Hullinger

Buzz Gator was at it again.

Buzz loved playing jokes on his good friend Cookie.

"Hee, hee, hee," he said to himself. "This is a great one."

"Very funny," said Cookie.

Buzz had glued her beautiful slippers together!

Cookie would not play jokes. Sometimes she wished she could.

"Come on! Laugh!" said Buzz.

That night Cookie did not sleep well. It seemed that night would never become day. It was so dark! In fact, it was even darker than dark.

After a long time, Cookie got up and stood on her porch.

It was bright! It was sunny! Buzz had painted her windows blacker than night.

"Good afternoon!" Buzz laughed.

"Buzz Gator," said Cookie. "You could become a pest."

Later, Cookie walked in the woods.
Buzz stood behind a tree nearby.
He put on a funny mask with a hood.
"This is great!" he said. "Beautiful! Hee, hee, hee!"
Then he heard footsteps. He didn't even look. He jumped into the path and waved his arms.
"Booooo!" he yelled in his loudest voice.

And there was the biggest, wildest bear he'd ever seen.

"Yipes! A great big bear!" Buzz cried louder than ever. Then he ran away— faster than he ever had in his life.

The next day, Buzz and Cookie were together again. "I'm sorry, Cookie. I should not have played those jokes on you," Buzz said.

"Oh, I don't mind," Cookie said.

"Maybe you'll play a good one on me someday," said Buzz. "And then we'll be even."

Cookie smiled. "Maybe I will," she said.

Moonbear's Pet

by Frank Asch

One spring day while playing in the pond Bear found
a new pet.

"Oh, what a cute little fishy!" cried his friend Little
Bird. "What will you call her?"

As Bear hurried home, he thought of names like Skinny, Sweetpea, and Slowpoke. But none of those names seemed quite right. Then he dropped his pet into a bowl of water and she landed with a *splash.* "That's it!" cried Bear. "We'll call her Splash!"

Bear and Little Bird loved to watch Splash swim and blow bubbles. They put Splash on the floor while they played and on the kitchen table while they ate.

After lunch they took Splash outside to watch while they worked in Bear's garden.

They even took Splash shopping!

Every night after Little Bird flew home to his nest, Bear stayed up late talking to Splash and telling her bedtime stories.

Every morning Little Bird brought Splash a
present: an acorn, a seashell, a pretty pebble, or
a pink button.

As the days and weeks passed

 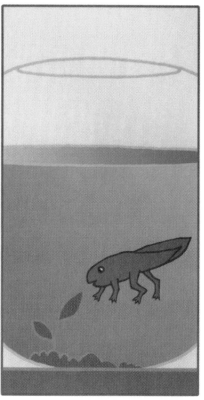

Splash grew bigger and bigger.

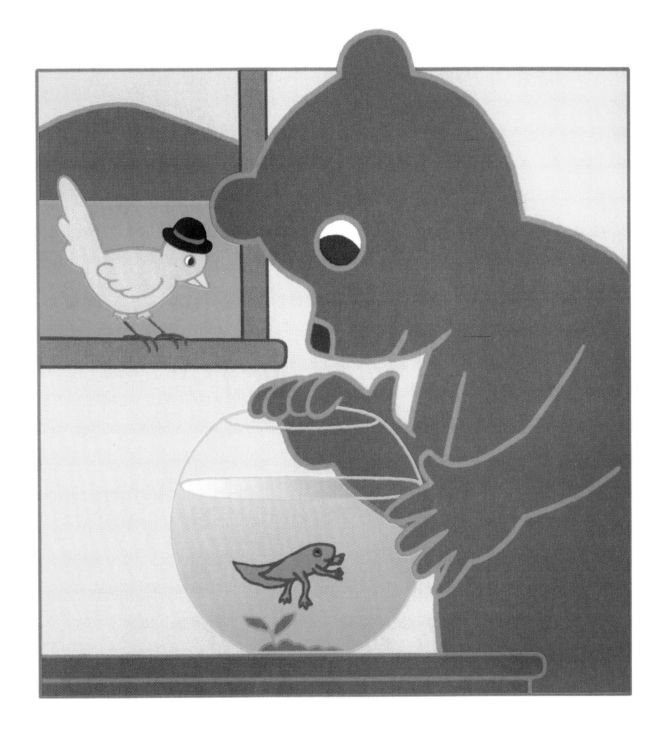

One day Little Bird chirped, "Look! Splash is growing wings. She must want to be a bird just like me!"

Bear took a close look at Splash. "Those aren't wings. See! There are four of them. They must be paws. Splash is becoming a bear just like me!"

"Why would anyone want to be a clumsy old bear when they could be a beautiful bird?" chirped Little Bird.

"Indeed!" exclaimed Bear. "Why would anyone want to be a chirpy sack of feathers when they could be a big strong bear?"

"Well, I guess we'll just have to let Splash decide for herself!" huffed Little Bird.

"That's just fine with me!" Bear huffed back.

So Bear and Little Bird put Splash in a tiny pool
next to Bear's pond and promised each other not to
visit her for a month.

"And don't visit me, either!" said Bear.

"I wouldn't dream of it!" snapped Little Bird.

Bear and Little Bird used to play together.

Now they played alone.

At the end of the month Bear and Little Bird met at Splash's pool.

"Now we'll see what a fine bear she's become," mumbled Bear.

"Or what a fine bird," grumbled Little Bird.

But Splash wasn't in the pool.

"Splash!" Little Bird called up to the sky.

"Splash!" Bear called into the woods.

Just then a young frog hopped up and croaked, "Here I am!"

"Please don't bother us now, little frog," said Bear. "We're looking for my pet, Splash!"

"But I'm Splash," said the frog.

"But you're not a bear!" said Bear.

"Or a bird!" said Little Bird.

"I was never a fish, either," said Splash. "I was a tadpole. And tadpoles don't become bears or birds. They become frogs!"

Bear was so surprised! All he could say was, "But wouldn't you rather be a bear?"

"I'd rather be a frog," said Splash.

"But wouldn't it be best if we were all birds?" said Little Bird.

"No," replied Splash calmly. "I think it would be best if we were all friends."

Bear was silent for a moment.

Then he said, "I think she's right."

"I agree," sighed Little Bird.

"I missed you, Little Bird," whispered Bear.

"I missed you too," Little Bird whispered back.

"And I missed both of you," cried Splash. "Come on! Let's all go for a swim!"

"Good idea!" said Bear.

"Great idea!" chirped Little Bird.

And they all jumped into the pond with a splash!

About the Author
Frank Asch

When Frank Asch was a child, he enjoyed nature. "I had a brook next to where I lived. I could catch frogs," he says. Mr. Asch has worked as a teacher. He has also acted with his wife in a children's theater group.

Mr. Asch loves writing for children. He believes that children bring out his "most interesting, most humorous ideas." He loves to make them laugh.

Reader Response

Let's Talk

What surprised you most in the story?

Think About It

1. How do Moonbear and Little Bird feel about Splash? How do you know?

2. Why does Moonbear tell Little Bird not to visit him anymore?

3. How do Moonbear and Little Bird become friends again?

Show and Tell

Find something important to you. Bring it in and show it to the boys and girls in your class.

Glossary

Words from Your Stories

Aa

across

across

The cat is walking **across** *the street.*

another

He asked for **another** *glass of milk. The hat didn't fit, so I chose* **another.**

apartment

An **apartment** is a room or group of rooms to live in: *There are ten* **apartments** *in that building.*

Bb

baseball

baseball

1 **Baseball** is a game played with a bat and ball. Two teams of nine players each play on a field with four bases.
2 A **baseball** is also the ball used in this game.

beak

beak

beak

beak

A **beak** is the hard part of the mouth of a bird. Another word for **beak** is **bill.**

beautiful

Beautiful means pleasing to see, hear, or feel: *We saw a* **beautiful** *swan. She had a* **beautiful** *plan.*

become

He has **become** *wiser as he has grown older. It has* **become** *warmer.*

best

Best means most excellent: *He's a good swimmer, but his brother is the **best** I've ever seen.* ● **good, better, best.**

between

*There is a big rock **between** the two trees. We'll be home **between** two and three o'clock.*

between

bottle

A **bottle** is something used to hold liquids. A **bottle** can be made of glass or plastic, and usually has a cap.

brain

The **brain** is the part of your body that is inside your head. You use your **brain** to learn, think, and remember. The **brain** makes it possible for you to talk, move, and see.

brain

brought

*He **brought** raisins in his lunch. We **brought** flowers for the teacher.*

bubbles

Bubbles are hollow balls of liquid floating in the air: **Bubbles** *rose up from the soapy water.*

Cc

cage

A **cage** is a box made of wires or bars. *Our pet bird sat in its **cage**.*

cage

camera

camera

camera

A **camera** is a machine for taking pictures or making videos, movies, or TV shows.

children

Children is the plural of **child**. Young girls and boys are **children**.

city

A **city** is a large town with many people living in it. New York and Dallas are **cities.**

clean

1 **Clean** means not dirty: *I wore* **clean** *clothes.*

2 When you **clean** something, you get rid of the dirt that is in it: *We will* **clean** *the kitchen.*

climb

climb

When you **climb**, you go up something: *Can you* **climb** *the ladder? The bikers* **climbed** *the mountain.*

complained

When you have **complained**, you have said that something is wrong: *The children* **complained** *about too much homework.*

could

She **could** *ski very well. Perhaps I* **could** *go with you tomorrow.* **Could** *we go to a movie?*

country

The **country** is the land away from the city: *There were many farms in the* **country.**

Dd

dashing

dashing

Someone who is **dashing** is running very fast: *The girls are dashing to the finish line.*

decide

Decide means to make up your mind: *I decide what to wear to school.*

dinosaurs

dinosaurs

Dinosaurs were animals that lived many millions of years ago. Some **dinosaurs** were bigger than elephants. Some were smaller than cats. No **dinosaurs** are alive today.

dumped

When something is **dumped**, it is emptied out: *I dumped the books out of the bag.*

Ee

easier

When something is **easier,** it is less hard to do or understand than something else: *She thinks math is easier than spelling. Tools often make our work easier.*

either

*Choose **either** of these toys to give to the baby.* **Either** *come in or go out. There are lights on* **either** *side of the driveway. If you don't go, she won't go* **either**.

elephant

elephant

An **elephant** is a large, heavy animal. **Elephants** have large ears and long trunks. They use their trunks to pick up things.

enemy

An **enemy** is anything that will do harm: *The snake was the mouse's* **enemy.**

enough

Enough means as much or as many as you need: *Are there* **enough** *sandwiches for all of us? My coat is not big* **enough.**

everywhere

I looked **everywhere** *for my gloves.* **Everywhere** *we went we met people we knew.*

exact

Exact means without any mistakes: *Only one group had the* **exact** *answer.*

exclaimed

When you have **exclaimed,** you have cried out with strong feeling: *"Oh, no!" she* **exclaimed** *as she dropped her ice-cream cone.*

explore

explore

Explore means to travel and to discover new places: *Astronauts* **explore** *outer space. The duckling set off to* **explore** *the pond.*

Ff

farm

To **farm** is to grow food or animals to eat or to sell: *I want to* **farm** *when I grow up.*

fix

To **fix** is to repair something that is broken: *Can you* **fix** *my watch?*

follow

Follow means to go or come after: *Let's* **follow** *him. Tuesday* **follows** *Monday.*

food

Food is anything that living things eat or drink. **Food** makes living things grow and gives them energy.

food

Gg

giggled

When you have **giggled**, you have laughed in a silly way: *The children* **giggled** *in the theater.*

guess

To **guess** is to try to give the answer to something when you are not sure: *She tried to* **guess** *before she looked up the answer. I* **guess** *it will rain tomorrow.*

Hh

have

I **have** *a nickel in my pocket. We* **have** *to go now. We always* **have** *breakfast in the kitchen. They* **have** *asked for their mail.*

hidden

hidden

Hidden means kept out of sight: *The story is about* **hidden** *treasure. The boy had* **hidden** *behind a big tree.*

high

high

High means up above the ground: *We walked up the* **high** *hill. The plane flew* **high** *in the sky.*

house

A **house** is a building where people or animals live: *She moved into a new* **house.** *I built a* **house** *for the birds.*

hundred

One **hundred** is the number after 99; 100: *There are one* **hundred** *cents in a dollar.*

Kk

keep

1 To **keep** is to have for a long time or forever: *She told me to* **keep** *the ring.*
2 To **keep** is to stay in good condition: *This coat will* **keep** *you warm.* ● **keeps, kept, keeping.**

knocked

If you have **knocked** something, you have hit it: *She* **knocked** *on their door.*

knocked

Mm

medicine

Medicine is something used to make a sick person well: *He took* **medicine** *for his cold.*

messages

1 **Messages** are information sent by one person to another: *I listened to my telephone* **messages.**
2 **Messages** are also sent from one place to another: *The eyes send* **messages** *to the brain.*

mirror

A **mirror** is a glass in which you can see yourself: *I checked my hair in the hand* **mirror.**

myself

*I can do it **myself**. I gave **myself** a haircut.*

Nn

need

If you **need** something, you are unable to do without it: *Plants **need** water to grow. I **need** new gloves for the winter.*

never

*He has **never** flown on an airplane. I will **never** get all of this work done.*

next

next

*She gave a flower to the girl **next** to her. I was sick on Monday, but returned to school the **next** day.*

Oo

order

An **order** is the way one thing comes after another in a special way: *Please line up in **order** of size to take your class picture. The words in a dictionary are in alphabetical **order**.*

outside

Outside is the opposite of inside: *The **outside** of the house needs painting. Please go **outside** and get the paper.*

Pp

paddle

paddle

Paddle means to move with the hands or feet in the water: *The duck likes to **paddle** around the pond.*

patch

A **patch** is a small piece of ground, often used to grow things: *He grows melons in the* **patch** *behind his house.*

paws

paws

Paws are the feet of an animal that has claws. Dogs and cats have **paws.**

peels

When something **peels**, the skin or covering is stripped off of it: *He* **peels** *the banana before eating it. The skin of some snakes* **peels** *off.*

pianos

Pianos are large musical instruments that you play with your fingers.

pile

pile

A **pile** is a heap, mound, or hill of something: *The truck dumped a* **pile** *of dirt.*

pitching

When you are **pitching**, you are throwing or tossing something, usually a ball: *She is* **pitching** *the ball back and forth with her sister.*

place

1 A **place** is the space where a person or thing is: *Our neighborhood is a nice* **place** *to live. Do not leave your* **place** *in line.*

2 A **place** is also a city, town, island, building, or other space: *We went to a* **place** *called Williamsburg. The auditorium is a big* **place.**

pleased

When you are **pleased**, you are happy or content with something: *He was* **pleased** *with his birthday presents.*

Qq

quiet

When something is **quiet** it makes no sound: *It was a* **quiet** *night.*

quite

There was **quite** *a change in the weather yesterday. It is not* **quite** *five o'clock.*

Rr

returned

If you have **returned**, you have come back: *They* **returned** *from their trip early.*

ripe

When something is **ripe** it is grown and ready to be picked and eaten: *We bought a bunch of* **ripe**, *yellow bananas.*

ripe

room

1 A **room** is a part of the inside of a building. Each **room** has walls of its own: *Please clean up your* **room**.

2 **Room** is also an amount of space that something takes: *There isn't enough* **room** *in the kitchen for everyone to sit down.*

Ss

scales

Scales are thin, hard pieces that form the outer covering of some fish, snakes, and lizards.

scales

sealing

If you are **sealing** something, you are closing it very tightly: *He is **sealing** the package with tape.*

should

*You **should** drink milk every day. I **should** have worn my boots.*

sick

sick

If you are **sick** you are feeling ill or not well: *He is **sick** and is staying in bed. I felt **sick** after riding the merry-go-round.*

since

*I have been up **since** dawn. He called twice **since** Monday. **Since** you are hungry, we can have dinner now.*

sometimes

***Sometimes** my aunt takes me to the zoo. I play with them **sometimes**.*

spray

A **spray** is a liquid that flies through the air in small drops: *When the dog shook itself, we all got damp from the **spray**.*

squeeze

squeeze

To **squeeze** is to push or press hard against something: *Will you **squeeze** the oranges to make juice? **Squeeze** these books onto the shelf.*

surface

The **surface** of something is the outside part of it: *The fish came to the* **surface** *of the water. A marble has a smooth, hard* **surface.**

surprised

When you are **surprised**, you didn't know that something was going to happen: *He was* **surprised** *by her call. He* **surprised** *his friend with a present.*

surprised

Tt

taste

Taste is the flavor something has when you put it in your mouth: *The* **taste** *of sugar is sweet.*

tears

Tears are drops of salty water that come from your eyes. **Tears** fall when you cry. This meaning of **tears** rhymes with **ears.**

tears

terrible

Terrible means causing great fear: *The* **terrible** *storm destroyed many homes.*

then

The noise stopped and **then** *began again. If he broke the dish,* **then** *he should clean it up.*

those

Those *are my books.* **Those** *toys are yours, and these are mine.*

through

The kitten ran **through** *the house. We learned a new song all the way* **through.** *She won the prize* **through** *hard work. Dad is* **through** *working every day at three o'clock.*

thumb

The **thumb** is the short, thick finger on each of your hands.

thumb

tomorrow

Tomorrow is the day after today: **Tomorrow** *it is supposed to be rainy. We'll get together* **tomorrow.**

tools

Tools are things that help you do work. Saws, hammers, rakes, and hoes are **tools.**

tools

toward

He walked **toward** *the door.*

 Uu

underneath

We sat **underneath** *the apple tree.*

until

She did not leave **until** *the following week. We waited* **until** *dark before we went in the house.*

use

When you **use** something, you put something into the action that it is meant for: **Use** *that umbrella to stay dry. We* **use** *scissors to cut paper.*

Ww

warm

Warm means more hot than cold. *I felt* **warm** *by the fire.*

wheel

A **wheel** is something round that turns on its center. **Wheels** help things move and work. A car has four **wheels.** *The mouse ran around a* **wheel.**

wheel

whole

1 When something is **whole**, it does not have anything missing: *I finished the* **whole** *puzzle. This is the* **whole** *class.*
2 **Whole** *also means in one piece: The dog swallowed the meat* **whole.**

world

world

The **world** is the Earth and everything on it.

write

When you **write**, you make letters or words with your pen, pencil, or chalk: **Write** *your name at the top of your paper.* ● **writes, wrote, written, writing.**

Tested Words List

Acknowledgments

Text

Page 12: *Franny and Ginny* © 1998 Pat Cummings.
Page 20: *Daddy, Could I Have an Elephant?* By Jake Wolf. Illustrated by Marylin Hafner. Text copyright © 1996 Jake Wolf. Illustration copyright © 1996 Marilyn Hafner. Reprinted by permission of William Morrow & Company, Inc.
Page 48: "Poppleton and the Grapefruit" from *Poppleton and Friends* by Cynthia Rylant. Illustrated by Mark Teague. Published by The Blue Sky Press, an imprint of Scholastic Inc. Text copyright © 1997 by Cynthia Rylant. Illustrations copyright © 1997 by Mark Teague. Reprinted by permission of Scholastic, Inc.
Page 62: "People" from *All That Sunlight* by Charlotte Zolotow. Text copyright © 1981 by Charlotte Zolotow. Reprinted by permission of S©ott Treimel New York.
Page 70: *Tools* by Ann Morris. Text copyright © 1992 by Ann Morris. Reprinted by permission of Lothrop, Lee & Shepard Books, a division of William Morrow & Company, Inc.
Page 94: *Three Little Bikers* by Tony Johnston. Text copyright © 1994 by Tony Johnston. Reprinted by permission of Writers House Literary Agency.
Page 124: "The Surprise" from *Frog and Toad All Year* by Arnold Lobel. Copyright © 1976 by Arnold Lobel. Reprinted by permission of HarperCollins Publishers.
Page 137: "Autumn Leaves" from *Just Around the Corner* by Leland B. Jacobs. Copyright © 1993 by Allan D. Jacobs. Reprinted by permission of Henry Holt and Company, Inc.
Page 138: (Haiku) "One by one..." and "Piles of ragged leaves..." from *Cricket Never Does* by Myra Cohn Livingston. Text copyright © 1997 Myra Cohn Livingston. Reprinted with the permission of Margaret K. McElderry Books, an imprint of Simon & Schuster Children's Publishing Division.
Page 148: *Duck (See How They Grow)* by Barrie Watts, photographer. Text copyright © 1991 by Dorling Kindersley Limited. Copyright © 1991 by Barrie Watts for photographs. Reprinted by permission of Lodestar Books, an affiliate of Dutton Children's Books, a division of Penguin Putnam Inc.
Page 174: "Seeing" from *You Can't Smell a Flower with Your Ear!* by Joanna Cole. Copyright © 1994 by Joanna Cole. Reprinted by permission of Grosset & Dunlap, Inc., a division of Penguin Putnam Inc.
Page 192: "Two Mice" from *Two Mice in Three Fables* written and illustrated by Lynn Reiser was originally published in *Images: Meet the Mammals* in *Heath Literacy* by Alvermann, et al. Copyright © 1995 by D. C. Heath & Company. All rights reserved. Reprinted by permission of Houghton Mifflin Company.
Page 208: *Snakes—All Aboard Reading* by Patricia Demuth. Illustrations by Judith Moffatt. Text copyright © 1993 by Patricia Demuth. Illustration copyright © 1993 by Judith Moffatt. Reprinted by permission of Grosset & Dunlap, Inc., a division of Penguin Putnam Inc.
Page 228: "Snake Problem" from *A Light in the Attic* by Shel Silverstein. Copyright © 1981 by Evil Eye Music, Inc. Reprinted by permission of HarperCollins Publishers.
Page 238: *Anansi and the Talking Melon* by Eric A. Kimmel & Janet Stevens. Text copyright © 1994 by Eric A. Kimmel. Illustrations copyright © 1994 by Janet Stevens. All rights reserved. Reprinted by permission of Holiday House, Inc.
Page 276: "Play Ball" from *Lionel and His Friends* by Stephen Krensky. Illustrated by Susanna Natti. Text copyright © 1996 by Stephen Krensky. Illustration copyright © 1996 by Susanna Natti. Reprinted by permission of Dial Books for Young Readers, a division of Penguin Putnam Inc.
Page 294: *People, People, Everywhere!* by Nancy Van Laan. Illustrated by Nadine Bernard Westcott. Text copyright © 1992 by Nancy Van Laan. Illustration copyright © 1992 by Nadine Bernard Westcott. Reprinted by arrangement with Alfred A. Knopf, Inc. and Nadine Bernard Westcott.
Page 322: *Wanted: Best Friend* by Ann M. Monson. Illustrations by Lynn Munsinger. Text copyright © 1997 by Ann M. Monson. Illustration copyright © 1997 by Lynn Munsinger. Reprinted by permission of Dial Books for Young Readers, a division of Penguin Putnam Inc.
Page 352: *Young Cam Jansen and the Dinosaur Game* by David A. Adler, illustrated by Susanna Natti. Copyright © 1996 by David A. Adler. Illustration copyright © 1996 by Susanna Natti. Reprinted by permission of Viking Penguin, a division of Penguin Putnam Inc.
Page 382: *Moonbear's Pet* by Frank Asch. Copyright © 1997 by Frank Asch. Reprinted with permission of Simon & Schuster Books for Young Readers, Simon & Schuster Children's Publishing Division.

Artists

John Sandford, cover
David Wenzel, 10
Fred Willingham, 12–19
Marylin Hafner, 20–39
Nan Brooks, 40–47
Mark Teague, 48–60
Deborah Morse, 62
Gregg Valley, 63
Seymour Chwast, 64–69
David Knipfer, 70–85
G. Brian Karas, 88–117, 402b
Maureen Fallows, 118a
Carla Siboldi, 118–123
Janet Ocwieja, 124a, 374a
Pamela Paulsrud, 124b, 136–138, 142a, 208d, 238b, 285c
Arnold Lobel, 124–135
Roberta Arenson, 138
Jerry Tiritilli, 140
Cheryl Kirk Noll, 142b–147
Christine Powers, 166–173
Neesa Becker, 174–181
Lynn Reiser, 192a, 193–201
Bobbi Tull, 192c, d
Mary Grand Pré, 202–207
Judith Moffatt, 208a–c, 209–226
Tracy Rea, 227, 229
Shel Silverstein, 228
Janet Stevens, 238a, 239–265
Loretta Lustig, 266
Mike Dammer, 267, 312–313, 400a, 405b, 409a, 411b, c
Jack Davis, 268–275
Susanna Natti, 276, 277b–284, 352–373
Jim Lange, 277a
Kevin O' Malley, 285a, 287, 404a, 408b, 411a
Tony Nuccio, 286a
Mike Sobey, 286b–286
Darryl Ligasan, 288–293
Nadine Bernard Westcott, 294–311
Bernard Adnet, 314–321
Lynn Munsinger, 322–343
Benton Mahan, 344–345, 401c, 407a, 410a, 412b
Donna M. Perrone, 346–351
Bradley Clark, 352b, c
Randy Chewning, 374b–375, 402a, 408a, 410b, 413a
C. D. Hullinger, 376–381
Frank Asch, 382–397
Pat Dypold, 398–399
John Zielinski, 400b
Brad Teare, 401a, 406b, 409b, 412a

Photographs

Page 61 (TL) © Carlo Ontal from *Best Wishes* by Cynthia Rylant, courtesy of Richard C. Owen Publishers, Inc., Katonah, NY

Page 61 (BR) Richard Hutchings for Scott Foresman

Pages 70–83 Ken Heyman/Woodfin Camp & Associates

Page 86 (TL) Courtesy Ann Morris

Page 86 (BR) Courtesy Ken Heyman

Page 108 (TL) Jack Pettee for Scott Foresman

Page 116 (CL) Courtesy Brian Karas

Page 129 Superstock, Inc.

Page 136 (TL) Courtesy, HarperCollins Publishers/Photo: Ian Anderson

Page 137 Superstock, Inc.

Pages 148–165 Images reproduced from *Duck (See How They Grow)* with permission of DK Publishing, Inc.

Page 182 (BC) Richard Hutchings for Scott Foresman

Page 192 (CL) Courtesy Lynn Reiser, Photo: Branka Whisnant

Page 230 (TL) PhotoDisc, Inc.; (CL) Simon D. Pollard/Photo Researchers; (CC) Larry West/Bruce Coleman Inc.; (CR) J. H. Robinson/Photo Researchers; (BG) © Orion Press/Natural Selection Stock Photography, Inc.

Page 231 (TL) John Serrao/Visuals Unlimited; (CL) Milton Rand/TOM STACK & ASSOCIATES; (BL) O. S. F. /Animals Animals/Earth Scenes

Page 232 (CL) James H. Carmichael/Photo Researchers; PhotoDisc, Inc.; (BR) J. H. Robinson/Photo Researchers

Page 233 (T) Charles McRae/Visuals Unlimited; (CR) David M. Dennis/TOM STACK & ASSOCIATES; (BR) Scott Camazine/Photo Researchers

Page 234 (TL) R. F. Ashley/Visuals Unlimited; (CR) Scott Camazine/Photo Researchers

Page 235 (CL) Norbert Wu/Tony Stone Images; (CR) Garry Walter/Visuals Unlimited; (B) Charles McRae/Visuals Unlimited

Page 236 (CL) Tom McHugh/Photo Researchers; (BR) Bill Beatty/Visuals Unlimited

Page 237 (TL) Larry West/Bruce Coleman Inc.; (TC) Joe McDonald/Animals Animals/Earth Scenes; (TR) Richard Walters/Visuals Unlimited; (BL) Larry Tackett/TOM STACK & ASSOCIATES; (BC) Sean Morris/O. S. F. /Animals Animals/Earth Scenes; (BR) Breck P. Kent/Animals Animals/Earth Scenes

Page 264 (TC) Eric Neurath for Scott Foresman

Page 285 (C) Frank Siteman for Scott Foresman

Page 312 (TL) Philip Greven; (CL) Courtesy, HarperCollins Publishers

Page 344 (CL) Courtesy Lynn Munsinger

Page 374 Courtesy Susanna Natti

Page 398 (TR) Courtesy Frank Asch

Page 403 David Young-Wolff/PhotoEdit

Page 404 PhotoDisc, Inc.

Page 407 Images reproduced from *Duck (See How They Grow)* with permission of DK Publishing, Inc.

Page 413 NASA

Glossary

The contents of the glossary have been adapted from *My Second Picture Dictionary*, Copyright © 1990 Scott, Foresman and Company.